WHEN TEACHING GETS
GETS

ASCD MEMBER BOOK

Many ASCD members received this book as a
member benefit upon its initial release.

Learn more at: **www.ascd.org/memberbooks**

WHEN TEACHING GETS
TOUGH

SMART WAYS TO RECLAIM YOUR GAME

ALLEN N. MENDLER

ASCD

Alexandria, Virginia USA

1703 N. Beauregard St. • Alexandria, VA 22311 1714 USA
Phone: 800-933-2723 or 703-578-9600 • Fax: 703-575-5400
Website: www.ascd.org • E-mail: member@ascd.org
Author guidelines: www.ascd.org/write

Gene R. Carter, *Executive Director;* Ed Milliken, *Chief Program Development Officer;* Carole Hayward, *Publisher;* Laura Lawson, *Acquisitions Editor;* Julie Houtz, *Director, Book Editing & Production;* Deborah Siegel, *Editor;* Georgia Park, *Senior Graphic Designer;* Mike Kalyan, *Production Manager;* Cynthia Stock, *Typesetter;* Sarah Plumb, *Production Specialist*

All web links in this book are correct as of the publication date below but may have become inactive or otherwise modified since that time. If you notice a deactivated or changed link, please e-mail books@ascd.org with the words "Link Update" in the subject line. In your message, please specify the web link, the book title, and the page number on which the link appears.

ASCD Member Book, No. FY12-6 (April. 2012, PSI+). ASCD Member Books mail to

Premium (P), Select (S), and Institutional Plus (I+) members on this schedule: Jan., PSI+; Feb., P; Apr., PSI+; May, P; July, PSI+; Aug., P; Sept., PSI+; Nov., PSI+; Dec., P.

Select membership was formerly known as Comprehensive membership.
PAPERBACK ISBN: **978-1-4166-1390-9**   ASCD product #**112004**
Also available as an e-book (see Books in Print for the ISBNs).

Quantity discounts for the paperback edition only: 10–49 copies, 10%; 50+ copies, 15%; for 1,000 or more copies, call 800-933-2723, ext. 5634, or 703-575-5634. For desk copies: member@ascd.org.

Library of Congress Cataloging-in-Publication Data

Mendler, Allen N.
   When teaching gets tough : smart ways to reclaim your game / Allen N. Mendler.
      pages cm
   Includes bibliographical references and index.
   ISBN 978-1-4166-1390-9 (pbk. : alk. paper)
   1. Effective teaching. 2. Teacher effectiveness. I. Title.
   LB1025.3.M48 2012
   371.102—dc23
                         2011047054

22 21 20 19 18 17 16 15 14 13 12 11 1 2 3 4 5 6 7 8 9 10 11 12

This book is dedicated to Barbara Mendler,

my wife, best friend, and great teacher.

It's been a great ride, and

it keeps getting better.

WHEN TEACHING GETS TOUGH

Acknowledgments

I'd like to thank the thousands of wonderful, talented, dedicated educators from every corner of the country and around the world who work every day to make a difference in the lives of students. It's doing the little things that makes for greatness: adapting lessons to accommodate diverse learners; showing interest; consoling a distraught student; recognizing something to make each of your students know he or she matters; refusing to settle for too little effort. You too often get little thanks and undeserved grief. I hope this book helps you realize and appreciate how special you are. In particular I want to thank the following teachers and schools for contributing meaningful ideas and strategies: Mr. Rogers at Sweetwater Middle School; Patricia Koefoed; Traci Martino; Alex McBean; M. T. Edmunds; Thomas Recigno; Jill Irons; Patricia McKitrick; Bellevue High School, Bellevue, Nebraska; and Rochester Charter High School, Rochester, New York. I want to thank many other educators who have attended my seminars or invited me to consult at your schools. In the process, I have learned a lot from you, and there are numerous strategies in the book that come directly from you or are adapted from ideas you have shared. Unfortunately, I don't always remember where I learned what, but thank you for enriching my professional life.

A special thank you to Laura Lawson, my nuts and bolts editor at ASCD, for your exacting feedback and suggestions. Thanks as well to Scott Willis and Carolyn Pool, who ushered me through the first phase of the book and who pushed me to get clear and focused on what I really wanted to say. I also wish to thank Nancy Modrak, publisher, for expressing interest in having me pursue this project. I have thoroughly enjoyed working with you for many years on a variety of projects. Your friendship and warmth has meant a lot, and I will miss you as you pursue the next phase of your life.

As always, to Rick Curwin, my closest and dearest lifelong friend and outstanding educator, I thank you for your careful reading of the manuscript and your important suggestions. Thanks as well to Brian Mendler, my son and educational consultant, for your feedback and your contribution of a few very important strategies. Your dedication to kids and teachers, your inspiring and motivational style of presentation, and your endorsement and furthering of my work has not only made me extraordinarily proud of you, it has revitalized my energy and commitment. To our other Teacher Learning Center consultants, Willeta Corbett, Jerry Evanski, Colleen and Dave Zawadzki, I thank you for your outstanding talent in communicating the Discipline with Dignity message to schools. Finally, thanks to Jon Crabbe, program director, Allison Yahtze, Erinn Drone, and the rest of the crew at The Teacher Learning Center for all you do on a daily basis to make things happen.

Introduction

For the Teacher

Are there days when you feel overwhelmed by some combination of unruly or poorly motivated students, parents who either give you a hard time or simply aren't to be found, and never-ending classroom distractions? Do you feel frustrated by burdensome meetings that accomplish little but eat up a ton of time? Are you getting tired pleading and scavenging for basic school supplies? Do you ever wonder if anybody notices or even cares how much effort you put out on a daily basis? Is there a knot in your stomach that tenses every time you hear faculty room chatter dominated by toxic colleagues bashing somebody or something? Do you often feel like a battered boxer, struggling to survive an onslaught of excessive paperwork and competing demands? Have you gotten to a point where you are fed up and think about quitting? Or have you emotionally left, but you hang on because you don't know what else to do and you need to pay the bills? If you answered yes to any of these questions, this book is written for you.

In my 35-plus-year career as a teacher and a school psychologist, I have worked with thousands of students from preschool through high school, including those with just about every label and acronym we have ever invented: LD, ED, BD, SBD, ADD, ADHD, ODD, PDD, and JD. I have sat in on innumerable discussions debating the pros and cons of virtually every literacy and curricula program there is, trying to decide where the dollars would best be spent. I have attended numerous conferences and read extensive research that touts one program or another as a superior way to increase student achievement and reduce behavior problems. In search of the best way to present curriculum, I have explored class size; traditional scheduling, block scheduling and modular scheduling; small-group instruction, large-group instruction, and individualized instruction; and reading labs, writing labs, and math labs. Frankly, what I have found is that with all the emphasis on using supposedly research-based teaching methods, virtually none of these methods really makes much of a difference. Little of what is emphasized actually connects to great teaching and learning. In fact, scholar and author John Goodlad, who looked at 40 years of educational innovations while at UCLA, did not find a single one that increased student achievement.

The only thing that increased student achievement was the effectiveness of the teacher (Goodlad, 1994). And students are most likely to succeed with teachers who know their stuff and can express themselves in an articulate way, convey confidence fearlessly, have a sense of humor, are well-organized, have high expectations, are willing to risk doing things differently when necessary, and realize they are as much performer as instructor. These teachers value listening to and connecting with their students, which enables them to push harder, and they refuse to give up when kids are giving up on themselves.

Teaching is tough. Very diverse classrooms with academically and behaviorally challenging students, limited parent or administrative support, blame for low test scores, and little say in curriculum decisions are but a few of the obstacles we face in being able to do our jobs as well as we possibly can. Virtually every piece of data on stressful occupations puts teaching at or near the top. While there are many ways to cope with stress, it is becoming increasingly common for teachers to simply get disgusted and leave. Some leave to teach at a different school, others to teach at a different level, and some to work at a different occupation. Perhaps even more of us leave psychologically, counting down the days until the end of the year. Some of us aren't well suited to the many demands and need to leave for our own well-being and the larger good.

It bothers me to lose great and potentially great teachers to the variety of frustrations that when handled differently can change dread to wow! Although there is no singular blueprint for all, there are many things you can do to improve your effectiveness (which is probably fine if you are a great teacher) and more importantly, your outlook (which is probably more negative than it should be). Most of the strategies covered in this book are entirely new, while a few are from prior books I have written. I like to think of this book as one resource that cuts right to the chase and offers excellent but overwhelmed teachers practical strategies that can be used right away to make things better. Each chapter also offers suggestions for administrators to help good teachers who are struggling. The book is purposely light on theory and rich with ways to regain enthusiasm and optimism. The goal is focusing on what works in an easy-to-read, easy-to-implement format to help you reclaim the feeling of satisfaction and sense of accomplishment that all teachers long for and deserve.

For the Administrator

Some school districts are currently experimenting with merit pay and other cash incentives to attract and retain their best teachers. Although the jury is still out on its effectiveness, common sense suggests that paying more is a tangible reward that provides obvious benefit to the recipient. Business works on this premise all the time. Yet even if all school districts paid their best teachers more money, there is ample research in the behavioral sciences literature that has shown money alone to be an insufficient incentive for sustaining top-notch performance. Favorable working conditions, appropriate challenge, support from colleagues, and recognition from above for a job well done are practices generally seen in organizations that are able to get and keep their best employees. As you well know, excellent teachers are a treasure that not only benefits your students but also makes your job easier. Great teachers are hard to come by, and it is obviously in the interest of every administrator committed to high achievement and happiness to do whatever is necessary to keep the best teachers satisfied, energized, and enthusiastic.

Researchers from around the country have attempted to examine every variable in schools that makes a difference in the achievement of students. Why is it that some teachers can regularly raise their students' test scores for children of the same race, class, and ability level while other teachers get below average results every year? Why do some teachers derive much better results than others who use the same reading or math program? How is it that some teachers can work magic with their students while others who teach the same kids struggle mightily? In an article in the New York Times Sunday magazine, Elizabeth Green (2010) shares data on the impact of effective teachers. Eric Hanushek, a Stanford economist, found that while the top 5 percent of teachers were able to impart a year and a half worth of gains in learning in one school year as assessed by standardized tests, the weakest 5 percent had students show only a half year of advancement each year. William Sanders, a statistician studying Tennessee teachers, found that a student with a weak teacher for three straight years, on average scores 50 percentile points behind a similar student with a strong teacher for those years. Zavadsky (2010) found that attracting and retaining effective teachers was one of five factors associated with significantly raised achievement and a narrowing of the achievement gap in urban schools. Clearly, these studies present severe limitations in exclusively linking teacher effectiveness to student performance on standardized tests. But in every school that has employed me or to which I consult, virtually every administrator, parent, student, and teacher can quickly identify the best teachers (these aren't always the ones that have the kids with the highest test performance) on request. These are virtually always the teachers that are able to get the best each student can give while considering a host of variables that impact learning.

Over the years, I have been privileged to observe what some of our best teachers do. In my other books, I have shared motivation and classroom management practices these teachers use to achieve success with difficult students. In this book, I share what teachers (and you) can do for themselves when some combination of difficult students, lack of adequate resources, and too little appreciation gets them down. Although this manuscript is written primarily as a self-help tool, your support as an administrator or resource person can be invaluable. For many excellent but stressed teachers, you can help by sharing some of the problem-solving strategies for such common issues as managing difficult students and challenging parents, differentiating instruction for classes filled with diverse learners while maintaining high standards for all, and finding alternatives when faced with inadequate materials. Most of the time, affirmation and appreciation for a job well done is all a good teacher really needs. Who better than you to provide this? You will find many suggestions throughout the book that you can use to make your teachers feel noticed, appreciated, and supported.

....

CHAPTER ONE

The Big Picture:
Attitudes and Strategies

If you want your life to be a magnificent story, then
begin by realizing that you are the author and every day
you have the opportunity to write a new page.

Mark Houlahan

I was recently consulting at an inner-city middle school and was asked to visit Ms. R's class, which was identified as one of the toughest. Apparently, the day before, she was practically reduced to tears due to their noncompliant behavior. Expecting the worst, I was surprised to find the students relatively well behaved. Many were involved in the interesting video of tornadoes that began the day's lesson, and then were very animated when the metaphor of an angry mother representing a tornado was presented by Ms. R. Kids talked openly about their relationships with their mothers, some expressing lots of love, others telling about how they boss their mothers around, while still others talked about preferring to be swept up by a real tornado rather than facing an angry mom.

About 35 minutes into the 45-minute period, Ms. R somehow connected the lesson to how she was feeling right then and expressed her delight at their positive behavior throughout the day's class. She told them that she actually felt like crying at the joy she was feeling. She then told them how different yesterday was, being very open about how upset she felt and how, as she left school the day before, she wondered why she even bothered to teach. As she went on with this for a few minutes, you could hear a pin drop in the classroom. Every single student was completely mesmerized by what they were hearing. A few minutes after she finished, some of her more difficult students began to revert back to their irritating behaviors.

Attitudes Are as Important as Strategies

The point of this story is that attitudes are at least as important as strategies when you are in difficult situations. Perhaps the two most important attitudes for teachers are:

1. Live each day as if there is no tomorrow
2. Understand that change is a roller-coaster ride

I observe many committed teachers lose their enthusiasm for teaching because they don't take it one day at a time. If you have a particularly difficult class or you are surrounded by too many toxic colleagues, it is easy to get discouraged and depressed if you start thinking about the many tomorrows that are ahead. Nobody in the midst of stress wants to think about how there are still six months left to the school year or 25 years to go until retirement. Teachers need every ounce of positive energy and enthusiasm they can muster. If things are tough, you might begin to think about other life options for yourself or apply for other jobs. Keep the door open to change, but approach each day as if there is no tomorrow. Only then will you have the grounding to live in the moment without being emotionally scarred with what happened yesterday. Take a second and look around. Volunteer with Special Olympics or Big Brothers/Big Sisters. Get outside your own little world and realize that while things are difficult right now, overall you have your summers off, never work weekends or holidays, have a very nice pension, and are blessed to have a career where you can drastically influence and change lives every day. As columnist Leonard Pitts Jr. writes (2011), "Get done what you came here to do, give the gifts you meant to give, do the good you're able to do, say what you need to say, now, today, because everything you see is temporary, the clock is ticking and the alarm could go off any second." Teach with BEEP—belief, energy, emotion, and passion every single day, as if it were your last on this beautiful Earth. Finally, realize that changing behaviors is almost always very difficult. It is a roller coaster ride of ups, downs, loops, and corkscrews. For the teacher, it is like being on the roller coaster blindfolded. Rarely do we know when the twists and turns will come. Virtually all people, including you and your kids, revisit old behaviors as they are acquiring new ones. It is quite likely that Ms. R's kids who started acting out after hearing her touching story were saying, "Don't expect me to be good always just because I've been good today. I'm not ready to be good always."

FISH!

The wonderful and highly effective FISH! program that guides employees at the Pike Market in Seattle, Washington, emphasizes four primary attitudes when treating customers and coworkers. Unlike any other store that sells fish, this one is special. For me, spending time in a store that sells fish would not normally be a priority. Yet this market is a fun place to be. Although it looks and smells like a fish market, it feels more like a playground for adults. Customers not only come to buy fish, but also see the market as a fun place to hang out. As described in the book *FISH! Tales* (Lundin, Christensen, Paul, & Strand, 2002), the fish philosophy is all about how employees should treat customers: *choose your attitude, play, make their day,* and *be present.* I believe these same attitudes are at the core of successful and satisfied teachers. The best teachers view their students as the most important customers they have.

Although most of the book is about strategies, we begin with attitudes since attitudes are the fuel that makes the engine go.

1. Play

Employees at Pike are encouraged, and in fact required, to have fun with each other and with their customers. It is not uncommon for employees to be cracking tasteful jokes and playfully tossing fish to customers and each other. They make time to play, bringing energy and fun along with commitment to the job.

At the Longaberger Company, a maker of handcrafted baskets and other home products in Newark, Ohio, there is an unwritten policy that employees are to take up to 25 percent of each work day having fun. If this practice was implemented in school, at least one and a half hours every day would be primarily about fun. When I interviewed a few employees to confirm this practice, one of them told me that when management tells employees that that they are having too much fun, it is not uncommon for an employee to answer, "I'm just getting in my 25 percent." Morale seems very upbeat there. Children do not question whether they should have fun; they just do it. Yet, if you ask one of your friends to do something just for fun, you are likely to hear, "I wish I could, but I'm too busy." Like an elite athlete who is not only talented in what he does but also loves doing it, satisfied teachers find ways to enjoy what they are doing and will often create their own fun. Look for ways to inject fun into as many things as you can while you teach. Laugh with your kids. Enjoy their quirky ups and downs. Revel in their youth, dreams, and naiveté.

2. Make their day

Employees are expected to take good care of their customers so they will want to come back. Within reason, employees do whatever they can to please the customer. Naturally, there are limitations. If customers come looking for produce in a fish market, they have to be redirected. Satisfied teachers know that their most important customer is the student. When students feel fulfilled, it makes our job a lot easier. Try to make everyone you come into contact with want to be around you. Take the advice of the noted business guru, Stephen Covey in *Seven Habits of Highly Effective People* and create an "emotional bank account" in which you "give before you get" (1989, p. 188). Ask yourself about everyone with whom you interact: how can I make their day? How can I make this person's life better? Because you are an excellent teacher, you likely do this naturally with most people anyway, but when our batteries are low, we tend to become more self-absorbed. It can help to think about a store or place you love to be. What happens that makes you want to be there? How do the people treat you? For most of us, the most important thing is to feel that others care about us. They notice us through a kind word or caring gesture, letting us know that we matter to them. Often, just some simple acknowledgment that lets each one know that you think he or she is special does the trick. A friendly greeting can go a long way. Making their day will usually make yours!

3. Be there

Employees are expected to be fully present: physically, emotionally, and behaviorally, tuning out distractions unrelated to their work so they are aware of what their customers are saying, thinking, and feeling throughout the day. One more quality is required for greatness as a teacher: passion. It is important to love what you teach and teach what you love so that your knowledge and energy comes as much from your heart as it does from your head. Passion inspires learning. By the time it is fifth period or later in the day, it is understandable that your energy might naturally be lower. So it may require a conscious effort to be on your game as much then as you were earlier in the day. More importantly, be there for yourself by appreciating what you are doing—even on days when no one else seems to care. Most days, you are the best person to congratulate yourself on a job well done. Recognize what you need and figure out the best way to get it. Try to remember that others are probably struggling even more than you are to feel good about what they are doing and about themselves. Therefore, they may not be giving you the support you need.

4. Choose your attitude

While events that happen are often beyond our control, how we react to the events is almost always within our control. This was evident during one of my visits to the fish market. An unsuspecting patron was hit in the face by a flying tuna. The worker/thrower was mortified as the customer cupped her face in her hands. After a few tense seconds, her hands lowered to show a face hysterically laughing. "I didn't know you guys actually throw the fish! That is so awesome. Trust me, I will be ready next time," she said. The attitude this woman chose made what would have been a tense situation into a laugh fest.

How do you react when an unsuspecting cuss word or incomplete homework assignment hits you in the face? Each and every one of us decides the attitude we take in every situation. We can and sometimes do blame others, events, or circumstances, but at the end of the day, we are the masters of our own fate. If you are up at 6:00 a.m. and feeling groggy, you can choose to be grumpy about it or you can get over it and remind yourself how lucky you are to have your health and the myriad of other fortunes that are easy to take for granted. Earlier, I wrote that one aspect of being a great teacher is performing or playing a role. Sometimes performers must act out a role even if it is not how they are really feeling. Sometimes this is necessary! Do you smile or scold when a student walks in late? Do you laugh or yell when a student calls you a name? Realize you don't always have to feel a certain way to act a certain way. We can choose how to be with our students, colleagues, and parents, no matter who they are or what they do. For example, try smiling even when you don't feel like it. You might notice that what you do can change the feelings you have. We can sometimes bring the emotion along by changing our behavior rather than waiting for the feeling to change. Attitudes can change feelings. You can choose to see someone as stubborn or strong-willed, lazy or easy-going, belligerent or persistent, threatening or challenging. The lens we look through determines what we see and affects how we react. Great leaders are able to rally people to a better future.

Teachers' Attitudes

There is a good likelihood that if you have been a successful teacher with a feeling of fulfillment, the above four attitudes are a reflection of who you are. You are either built this way or you have learned well from others. Your success can be attributed to the fact that teaching has enabled you to be playful and present for your students. Although things haven't always gone your way, you have felt in charge of who you are and what you do. Your greatest satisfaction has come from seeing the glow on the face of the kid who finally gets it, the relief from the burdened student who trusts you enough to confide in you, and the fun you experience when you go to your place of work realizing that an important part of your job requires you to think, feel, and sometimes even act like a kid. Just as likely, if there are growing doubts about whether teaching remains the right career for you, one or more of these attitudes is being chipped away by people, events, or circumstances that may or may not be directly within your control. Keep in mind that changes in behavior often *precede* changes in beliefs, attitudes, habits, and expectations (Kotter & Cohen, 2002; Fullan, 2007). As noted by Patterson, Grenny, Maxfield, McMillan, and Switzler (2008), the change process begins by asking, "In order to improve our existing situation, what must people actually do? (p. 26)" A good place to start reclaiming your enthusiasm is to recognize how your thoughts, expectations, or behaviors are getting in the way and then figure out what you can actually do to change them.

Four Major Challenges and Strategies to Deal with Them

After my many years of observing, counseling, and advising teachers, four major issues stand out as factors that lead to teacher dissatisfaction. Each section of the book addresses one of these challenges. All contain problem-solving and coping strategies to keep you energized or reawaken your BEEP (belief, energy, enthusiasm, passion).

1. Difficult, disruptive, or unmotivated students with or without a sense of entitlement

By far, the most frequent complaint among teachers is disruptive or unmotivated students. Effectiveness as a teacher and feelings of satisfaction can often be derived by focusing on six factors:

- Relationship
- Relevance
- Responsibility
- Success
- Safety
- Fun

The more you are guided by these six characteristics in your curriculum and in your interpersonal moments with students, staff, and parents, the better your chances are of having motivated and well-behaved students. Because teachers spend the bulk of their time with students, when students want to learn and want to behave, most teachers feel fulfilled and are happier. Although it is not the only cause of burnout, without question, unruly, unmotivated students is the number one cause for most teachers. Because of this, many strategies (which I will explain in Chapter 2) focus on how to deal with difficult students and manage your classroom most effectively. Chapter 2 also provides practical strategies to make your classroom a place where both you and your students want to be.

2. Little support and appreciation from colleagues, administrators, and parents

There are few tangible external rewards available to teachers. Virtually all teachers make the same money and receive the same benefits, which are based on seniority rather than merit. It is amazing that even the best teachers are rarely noticed by administrators, thanked by parents, appreciated by colleagues, or recognized by their pupils for the myriad of things they do to enrich the lives of their students. In fact, those teachers who become the best at working with the hardest to reach students are often rewarded by being given even more such students with no more support or resources. If that wasn't enough, too often adults who should be supportive and appreciative are irritating and blaming. You will learn how to seek support from others, but more importantly how to provide your own self-nourishment regardless of the environment around you. Chapter 3 contains strategies to defuse hostile parents, colleagues, and administrators.

3. Lack of resources to do the job most effectively

Availability of resources varies by school and by district, with wealthier schools usually having an abundance of the best supplies and materials while less wealthy schools often struggle to provide updated textbooks to students. In some schools, it is not unusual for teachers to change classrooms each period, making it extremely difficult to keep organized. Some schools have a bright, cheery feel of openness due to updated construction, sun-splashed vaulted ceilings and brightly decorated walls, while others look like condemned institutions.

One of the challenges some of us face is how to access more materials when we need them and how to brighten a dreary environment. Additional resources for teaching are often best secured through enhanced professional development opportunities. Like great doctors, great teachers need continuous training to keep abreast of the latest pedagogical methods and technological advances. Yet with schools always subject to the vagaries of the larger economy, professional development is one of the first things to go when budgets are tight. Complicating matters, the presence of inane policies and unrealistic expectations are often enough to drive away some of our best. Chapter 4 explores how to secure the best resources you can and survive the rancor of misguided policies, procedures, and expectations that can steer even the best teachers off course and make them want to throw in the towel.

4. Inability or unwillingness to make yourself a priority

There is only so much that individual teachers can do to change the system or other people. It may be human nature to think that the "grass is always greener." However, when we get up close to the other side, we often realize that the grass is just as green or brown there as it was in the place we just left. There are certainly exceptions, but if you are good at what you do yet you are feeling stressed out or disillusioned, it may be that teaching is a great fit for you, but you need to take better care of yourself.

Great teachers are notoriously good at nurturing others but not necessarily good at nurturing themselves. A top-notch teacher needs to take top-notch care of herself to remain top-notch. This can be accomplished through physical exercise, better nutrition, and healthy activities that can calm your mind. Fortunately, there is much you can do to enliven and reawaken your own spirits that is largely independent of your surroundings. Chapter 5 offers healthful activities for the mind and attitude adjustment strategies that will help keep you level-headed and emotionally responsive even when you can't directly change the people or circumstances around you.

The book is designed for each of the subsequent chapters to stand on its own. You do not have to read one to benefit from another. So move about depending on what you suspect is the biggest obstacle to satisfaction for you and explore, learn, and practice those strategies. For example, if you primarily find yourself dissatisfied over a lack of support from colleagues or administrators, go right to Chapter 3.

⑦ Questions for Reflection

1. If the road to satisfaction is *choose your attitude, play, make their day,* and *be present,* on a scale of 1–5, where do you rank on each measure?

2. What are the obstacles at school or in your mind that prevent you from moving in the direction of any or all of these attitudes? Can you think of any ways to address these obstacles?

3. If there was one new thing that you had to do tomorrow to further fulfill each attitude, what would it be?

4. Four main issues have been identified as the leading cause of stress and burnout for teachers. On a scale of 1–5, rank each issue according to how you are affected by it.

1. Disruptive/Unmotivated students
   Not a problem   1 --- 2 --- 3 --- 4 --- 5   Source of great stress

2. Lack of appreciation from colleagues, administrators, and parents
   Not a problem   1 --- 2 --- 3 --- 4 --- 5   Source of great stress

3. Inadequate resources
   Not a problem   1 --- 2 --- 3 --- 4 --- 5   Source of great stress

4. Lack of attention to yourself
   Not a problem   1 --- 2 --- 3 --- 4 --- 5   Source of great stress

Your responses to this informal survey can give you a good idea about where to go within the book for strategies and ideas. Obviously, the higher the source of personal stress this issue is for you, the more likely you will be to benefit from the strategies in the section that addresses the issue.

Key Chapter Thoughts

- Live each day as if there is no tomorrow and understand that change for you and others is a roller coaster ride.
- Play and have fun. For example, try smiling even when you don't feel like it. Make a point of saying or doing at least one thing you enjoy each period.
- If you strive to make *their* day fulfilling, there is a really good chance that you will make your own day satisfying.
- Be there. It may require a conscious effort to be more on your game with some of your students, classes, parents, colleagues, and administrators. It is ultimately worth the effort. More importantly, be there for yourself by appreciating what you are doing even on days when no one else seems to care.
- Choose your attitude. The lens we look through determines what we see and affects how we react.

For the Administrator

Ours is a people business. With all the talk about the need for high standards, a challenging curriculum, relevant instruction, 21st century skills, professional learning communities, and innovation through technology, running an effective school is about establishing a climate where teachers want to teach and students want to learn. It is people who bring about change for better or worse, and your best teachers are already making things happen. This doesn't mean that you shouldn't want or expect your best teachers to get even better. As new approaches develop to help students learn at high levels, even the best teachers will need to embrace change. However, the last thing you want is for the latest mandate, initiative, or vision to be a source of irritation and stress. Since your best teachers already have what it takes, your goal should be figuring out ways to get more teachers to act like them.

When there is a desire or mandate for a new initiative, think about ways your best teachers can get behind this initiative with the same verve and skill they bring to their classrooms. Realize that new initiatives should be presented, initiated, and evaluated while furthering the four key attitudes among your best teachers and hopefully awakening these same attitudes in those less capable: choose your attitude, play, make their day, be present. As the school leader, you should encourage all teachers to behave in ways that reflect these four attitudes in order to establish or reinforce a school climate that provides the energy and creativity essential to the teaching-learning process.

When change is on the horizon, give your best teachers a "heads-up." I have noticed that it is often the best teachers who are most bothered by mandated curricula or schedule changes. Sometimes they simply disagree with what has changed, but more often they are resentful at having had no say. To paraphrase Saphier (2005), virtually never will they disagree with goals that articulate a crystal clear curriculum that includes a compact list of learning intentions and success criteria. They may have issues pertaining to curriculum content, the specifics of the learning goals, or how to best measure mastery. Seek their involvement and their ideas about how implementation can best happen with the least amount of disruption. If there is disagreement, uncertainty, or confusion, provide clarification. Kotter and Cohen (2002) point out, "In a change effort, culture comes last, not first" (p. 175). Culture changes after people change. The more you can get your best teachers behind a new initiative, the more likely this initiative will become a permanent part of the school's fabric.

....

CHAPTER TWO

Strategies for Working
with Difficult Students

*When you're screwing up and nobody says anything to
you anymore, that means they've given up on you.*

Randy Pausch, author of *The Last Lecture*

Dealing with difficult students is the number one cause of burnout for most teachers. These students can be obnoxious, annoying,
irritating, and very hard to like. Few teachers enjoy waking up in the
morning and feeling like they are about to enter a war zone. Continued exposure can easily lead to emotional surrender. Teaching is
obviously much more enjoyable when students behave and are eager
to learn. Sadly, the lack of outside family and community support
coupled with an expectation of entitlement without effort are powerful forces that can impair our ability to influence student behavior.

Six Pillars for Success

Often, we can dramatically increase our influence with students
through strategies that are compatible with the curriculum and
with our interpersonal moments. The strategies are guided by six
"pillars for success":

- Relationship
- Relevance
- Responsibility
- Success
- Safety
- Fun

Relationship

This is about creating or revising your classroom so that it is a warm, welcoming, supportive place where all feel a sense of community. In his book *BLINK*, Gladwell (2005) cites research by Levinson in which malpractice lawsuits against physicians were studied. The findings indicated that doctors who are sued make no more mistakes than doctors who aren't sued. What matters is the relationship between the patient and the doctor. Doctors who spent 20 percent more time with their patients were much less likely to be sued than doctors who spent less time with their patients. These patients whose doctors spent time with them felt their doctor cared about them. I don't think it is much of a stretch to assume that if a simple act of caring and listening can prevent medical malpractice lawsuits, these same qualities shown by a teacher to her students and their parents is likely to favorably influence student behavior. Most teachers I know care deeply about their students. Yet many students I have interviewed have told me that they don't believe they would be missed by their teachers if they didn't come to school. Perhaps we need to be more demonstrative in showing the caring that is in our hearts. Make it a top goal to be a cheerleader for your students, particularly those students whose actions make others want to turn away from them. Create a classroom climate where students help and even "cheer" for each other.

One simple thing you can do to get started is to have students finish these sentences:

One thing I do well at school and if asked I could help somebody else with is _____ .

One thing I do well at home and if asked I could help somebody else with is _____ .

A strength most people don't know about me is _____
_____ .

When I need help I _____ .

Their answers can become the foundation upon which students look out for each other. Younger children can draw their answers.

Marion, a 3rd grade teacher I know, uses a "Mystery Person" strategy. She draws a name card and places it in a sealed envelope. The class will earn a reward if the person whose name was selected behaved well during the day. The teacher only reveals the student's name if a reward was earned and the student is okay with others knowing. That is important because publicizing a student when he has not achieved a reward for the class can lead to bullying. Marion uses this as one of her strategies to get others to like students who are not popular, so she makes sure that they are selected more often. Because she picks the card and puts it in the envelope, she is the only one who truly knows the name of the child selected.

Relevance

A frequent complaint from students when we are teaching subject matter content is "When are we going to ever use this?" Many students fail to see the relevance between our content and their lives. When they don't, they become bored and uninterested. Make it a goal to begin each class with a connection between what you are going to teach and something that your students can relate to. For example, when Martin Luther King Jr.'s birthday is about to arrive and you teach math, you might begin a lesson with the question, "What did Martin Luther King Jr. and algebra have in common?"

(Answer: equality). By the way, I want to thank my colleague Rick Curwin for that example. If you cannot find a way to make the lesson relevant, at least connect with your students for a few seconds every day around something you know they find interesting (Hint: music, sports, video games, and money are virtually always of interest to kids).

When I worked with juvenile delinquent adolescent boys in a lock-up facility, most behaved as if they could not care less about their education. Most were not interested in seeing how a good education would benefit them. This began to change when I told them how much more money they were likely to make with a high school diploma than without one. Nowadays, the median difference in income between a high school dropout and a high school graduate is about $8,000 per year; there is a $16,000 annual difference when comparing high school dropouts' income with that of those who have some college; there is a $21,000 difference in comparison with a college graduate, and a $40,000 per year difference in comparison with those who hold an advanced degree. In a 30-year work life, that amounts to nearly a quarter of a million dollars just between a high school graduate and a dropout (U.S. Census Bureau, 2009). After I shared this data with them, I saw many of their faces light up when they realized that they could buy thousands of cool sneakers, DVDs, numerous cars, and other valued items with that money.

Responsibility

Kids are not born responsible. This is a skill they need to learn. The best way to learn responsibility is to practice making choices and decisions, and then experiencing the consequences of those decisions. Many students with chronic school problems have become turned off to school and don't care about the consequences we give them. Most do better when we listen and ask rather than demand and tell.

Telling, ordering, and threatening do not teach responsibility. At best, they get kids to obey, which does not teach them how to make good choices in the absence of authority. Unfortunately, many students who misbehave have not learned responsibility at home. They are being raised either without limits or with inflexible limits. The former situation provides kids too many choices or choices they are not ready to handle. The latter case gives kids few if any opportunities to make decisions. It is obviously much more difficult for teachers to teach responsibility when parents don't, yet if our students aren't learning at home, there really is no choice but to emphasize this crucial skill at school. The best ways to promote responsibility are with involvement, ownership, and choices with limits. (For example, "You can answer any five that best show me you understand the main causes of the Civil War or you can create a song with clean lyrics that includes the main causes.")

Our students need us to get them involved in making decisions about as many things as they can. Although it may be easier to tell them, try to avoid immediately giving them your solutions or consequences and instead ask questions leading them to think on their own. Find ways to give your students choices they can handle, celebrate with them when their choices work out, and hold them accountable when they make mistakes. For example, "Jose, it looks like you thought you could get by without doing any work. The results of your test show that that strategy didn't work out. So let's look at what you can do to get the practice we both know you need to be more successful. I have a few ideas (don't share them right away), but I bet you do as well (encourage students to first come up with their own solutions and then try to help them anticipate what the consequences of their choice might be). What do you think?" If Jose doesn't know or won't participate, conclude by telling him what you will do in the absence of his involvement, but keep other options available. (For example, "Unless and until I hear differently from you, I will plan to call home to discuss some solutions with your parents. If you have any other ideas that you think will work better, please let me know by the end of the day.")

In addition to doing the right thing for oneself, responsibility grows when it is expected that students will look out for each other. For example, bullying can be significantly curbed when "bystanders" (especially students who are leaders) neither ignore nor join in, but instead confront the bully together with "We don't do that here." Have them practice confronting the bully as a group to show them how responsible actions by the group can influence an individual. Help them see how the actions of others affect them. For example, "Too much time is being wasted with reminders to pay attention and socializing during project time. Who has some ideas about how to fix this so that we don't need to cancel the field trip?"

Responsibility flourishes when we put students in situations where they are in charge and allow them to make decisions they can manage. We developed a program for the locked-up students mentioned earlier where the boys were paired with severely disabled kids from a local school. The students in lock-up became "helpers" and "friends" to the disabled kids. In the process, they bonded very quickly with their disabled buddies and showed patience, encouragement, and persistence while working with them. For the first time in many of their lives, they were helping instead of being helped. This is a powerful strategy for transforming both groups of kids. There are a lot of kids who need to know that they matter, and some will provoke others until they learn a different way.

Success

Nobody starts school expecting to fail. Yet failure is probably the number one in-school factor that causes students to become disaffected, uninterested, unmotivated, and disruptive. Try to make grades dependent more upon effort than ability. Every day, challenge your students to get better than they were yesterday in your subject matter. Make that the standard for success. For example,

"You got the first three correct and that is good. I am proud of you. But let's see if you can get four correct tomorrow. Good luck." Create and modify assignments, quizzes, tests, and behavioral expectations based upon this premise.

Great teachers seek out success. Instead of pointing out that a student got a 60 percent on a quiz, circle the six out of ten he got right. Then do whatever it takes, which may include looking beyond the curriculum guide and creating or borrowing methods that may be different from the ones that have failed. If a student is interested in football, use touchdowns while teaching multiplication. If a student gets fidgety quickly, hand her a soft rubbery object to fiddle with. The attitude of a great teacher is "You will succeed because you can. You learned to walk even though you fell down many times at first. You learned to talk even though at first other people couldn't understand what you were saying. So don't ever expect me to give up on you and never give up on yourself." Praise them when they do well, with your focus being on the effort and the strategy they used. For example, "Carter, you did well because you kept at it and tried three different ways to solve the problem." Stay away from praise for factors over which they really have no control (e.g., "See, you did well because you are so smart"). Praise yourself as well (e.g., "I got through to Laurie because I took the time to focus on her interests").

Let your students know that it will be tough for them to fail your class if they follow three Ps: *prepare, plan,* and *practice.* Show them how these look and sound, because these strategies may be different in your class than in other classes. Provide follow-up with those who need it by teaching them these skills. Encourage or require your students and yourself to keep a daily "success journal." What successes made you feel proud? What did you accomplish today? How did you get better today than you were yesterday? Elementary teachers can do this each day for the last 15–20 minutes of class. Middle and high school teachers might do this the last 5–6 minutes of class two or three times per week. Each student writes down three specific successes that made him feel proud or good about himself. The teacher can be creative here. You might have students write down a success they noticed one of their peers having. Maybe the students can write down successes they noticed the teacher having. As with most strategies, there are tons of ways to adapt it to fit your style.

Remember, your goal is to get across the idea that you have much more control of the process than you do of the outcome. You can't control your genes, but you can control what you do with them. You can't control what the pitcher throws, but you can practice hitting different pitches. When prepare, plan, and practice is the success mantra, students will virtually always be able to see themselves getting better.

Safety

Kids do best when they feel their teacher is in charge. There are many ways to convey leadership while being respectful of your students as people with opinions that may differ from yours. One way is to connect rules and consequences to values and principles. When students know not only what the rules are but why we want them to follow the rules, they are usually more compliant. For example, "Saying and doing things that are intended to hurt someone physically or mentally is not acceptable" is a rule that should be guided by the value of safety and learning. The explanation goes something like, "When somebody's mama gets called a nasty name, not only is that a disrespectful thing to say, but whoever got called the name is probably not going to be able to concentrate on doing math. And math is tough enough even when all of our brain cells are working rather than thinking about how we're going to get back at that person. That's why there is no name-calling allowed. Who's got some ideas about some consequences just in case somebody forgets?" Responsibility and safety are both promoted when students are invited to join in developing rules and consequences based upon the values you know are necessary in order for good learning and good teaching to occur. Rules are respected and followed when they are guided by specific expectations that help protect students from others who may want to get in the way of their dreams.

Fun

The more you enjoy doing what you do, the more students will *want* to be around you. Enthusiasm is contagious, so be animated when you teach and have fun with your students and with the curriculum. Laugh with them! A music teacher at one of my seminars in Houston shared that when he senses his kids getting bored or fidgety, he has them stand in a circle and laugh with a partner for one continuous minute. In addition to being fun, this helps his students become less active and more centered. There are lots of ways to make your class pleasurable, but be sure to make a habit of doing or sharing at least one story, experience, or factoid every day that is fun for you. Against a backdrop of fun and pleasure, students are much more forgiving when a unit is dull and boring. You can even add an element of fun to a boring lesson by announcing in advance how boring the unit is likely to be. Don't hide it from them. Tell your students that you will do your best to make it interesting, but it's one of those things that can be tough to learn for reasons that are hard to explain. Conclude with something like, "We've got to get through it because it is going to be on the state test at the end of the year, and unless you want to see me again next year in the same class, you need to know it." If boredom sets in, allow for some brief "moan and groan" time. Permit yourself to be one of the loudest! They'll love it when you show that you can out-groan them.

Three Roles

Yuen (2005) describes three roles parents need to embody: *ruler, teacher,* and *friend*. Perhaps with slight modification, I believe teachers need to model the same three roles in order to be effective with kids. The benevolent *ruler* is needed when students do or threaten behavior that can have dire consequences. Certain things are nonnegotiable, like doing something dangerous or giving up. At those times firmness in the form of "my way or the highway" is necessary. The *teacher* is needed to teach students how to behave and what to learn to be successful. The *friend* is there to support them during tough times and be playful with them to share and celebrate. Some teachers might argue that being friendly is fine, but being a friend crosses the line. I prefer to think of *friend* as a person who is there when support is needed rather than someone who hangs out with you socially.

As you read on, think of when and how drawing upon these three roles might be necessary for you. The remainder of this chapter contains many strategies that can have a positive influence on the behavior of difficult students. They are grouped into two categories: *prevention* and *intervention*. All of the strategies are designed to further one or more of the six pillars and each strategy asks you to be some combination of teacher, ruler, and friend.

Prevention Strategies

There are many strategies that can prevent occurrences or reoccurrences of problem behavior. Because the number one issue that gets great teachers to doubt their competence is the challenge to successfully and consistently manage difficult behavior, you will find these strategies very helpful in giving you ways to connect with tough kids and motivate them to want to learn. Like a great athlete who pushes even harder when the competition stiffens, getting to or staying at the top of your game can only be achieved when the tough kids become more interested in learning than they are in disrupting. As you read each strategy, consider how you might use it or an adapted version. There are some strategies that will be a better fit for you than others, so use your judgment to pick and choose those you think would be most effective for you.

Be in charge

My colleague and good friend Colleen Zawadzki, who also happens to be a black belt in karate, once told me that the secret to success with the toughest kids is to act as if you own the sidewalk and are preparing to buy the other side. It is not necessary or even desirable to be mean, but it is good to come across as confident and in charge so that your students will both respect you and experience a touch of fear as well. Many studies have found that nonverbal communication, which includes tone of voice and body language, is much more powerful than words. Focus on standing upright, making clear but not prolonged eye contact (five seconds is usually about right), and speaking clearly, slowly, and specifically. If this is difficult at first, it can help to have an image of someone who projects considerable confidence to you and imagine you are this person when you are giving directions or correcting a student. You might identify a few of the teachers at your school who seem to have little trouble gaining the respect of their students. Study them. Watch to see how they give directions, establish expectations, and correct behavior. Ask to visit their classes and watch how they interact with the students.

Have clear, specific procedures

To foster a smoothly functioning classroom, be very clear about the procedures you expect your students to follow. Among other things that may be specific to your subject, these should include how to enter the classroom, where to find the assignment, what to do if a pencil breaks, how to get permission for a drink or to use the bathroom, how to walk through the halls, how to line up, and how to take turns. It is important that these procedures be both explained and practiced. When you notice a procedure being followed well, point this out. Reinforcement always helps. Similarly, if you see one not being followed, get at it right away. Use these moments as opportunities to teach what you need the students to learn. Review your procedures approximately once per month.

Perhaps the most important procedure that relates specifically to difficult student behavior is to let all your students know that it will be rare for you to stop class to handle somebody's misbehavior for two reasons:

1. You have no interest in either embarrassing the student or yourself.

2. You will not sacrifice important instructional time to handle misbehavior.

Let your students know that almost always you will see the student after class or during a more private moment, and it will be then that you will either give a consequence or otherwise figure out a solution with the student. Tell your students something like this:

> If and when somebody breaks a rule, it may look as if I am ignoring what they did. I don't ignore bad behavior, but I am not always going to stop class to deal with it because that would waste too much time and might possibly embarrass the student. So understand that if you break a rule, there are consequences, but most of the time, those will be given after class or when it won't take away from everybody's learning.

Too often, challenging students seem intent on dominating class time with their unacceptable behavior, and it is therefore very important that you not give in to this. When something happens that warrants a consequence, say something like this:

> I know you all just saw what Ethan did, and most of you are probably wondering what I am going to do about it. Later on, Ethan and I will figure this out, but right now, we are on page 15.

Then get back to instruction.

Transition from the weekend

In response to the question "How was your weekend?" one of my students became distraught and shared that her sister had been raped. Another boy talked about a shooting on his street. Weekends can be an especially difficult time for kids who live in dangerous neighborhoods or who have lousy home lives. Even well-adjusted students appreciate a few moments devoted to sharing and hearing about each other. Begin the week by spending 10 to 12 minutes transitioning from the weekend to the week. Give your students a chance to share their experiences or fears before launching into the week's work. For some classes, a daily dose of this suggestion is needed.

Good questions to use as openers are:

- What is one thing you did, saw, or heard this weekend that was interesting?
- Who would like to share something important that happened to them?
- Is there anything that happened that made you feel happy? Sad? Mad? Scared?
- What is something you did that made you feel proud? Disappointed?
- What would make you feel even more proud?

Many additional questions appropriate for discussion with kids can be found in Gregory Stock's, *The Kids' Book of Questions* (2004).

Work twice as hard to connect with irritating students

Throughout my training in education and psychology, nobody ever told me there was a strong likelihood that I would dislike certain students. So it came as a shock when I discovered that I didn't like some of my kids. In fact, there were even a few I couldn't stand! I remember mentally beating myself up at first, thinking that I was a lousy teacher. Fortunately, I took a risk and shared these feelings with an older teacher who I greatly respected. Without batting an eye, Ms. Samuels looked at me and said, "When you don't love a student, make a commitment to love them twice as hard. Realize that last year's teacher didn't love this child enough, so you have to not only give for yourself but for last year's teacher as well." This same mentor teacher then told me that all of the best teachers need to have a "touch of multiple personality disorder." She explained that just like in life where it is entirely normal to like some people more than others, there will be some students you will like more than others.

Unlike the "real world" where you can simply distance yourself from those you don't like, as a teacher, you don't have the luxury to disengage from these students. In fact, they are the ones who need you the most. So begin by recognizing your feelings, and if you need to yell, scream, or do some other type of cathartic release (in private), go ahead, but at the end of the day, your job is to make school a welcoming place for even your most difficult students. With this in mind, I offer a simple daily welcoming strategy for you to use with all of your students but especially with those who make themselves hard to like. Greet them every day with one of these four Hs: *Say hello, ask "how are you?," give a handshake, or high-five.* Learn a welcoming statement in all languages represented in your classroom (i.e., Nice to see you; How's it going?) and share your greeting as students arrive. Most teachers are amazed at the mileage they get when they remember to do the little things. If yesterday was a tough day, start today fresh: "We had a tough day yesterday, but today is a new day. Good to see you!"

At a seminar I gave at an elementary school in Houston, one of the teachers talked about a boy in her class from the year before who had been driving her crazy. She shared with staff that she was determined to "love him even more" as her primary way to help him change his behavior. She initiated an "I need a hug" ritual by telling him that because she had no son at home to hug, she needed a little boy to hug every day to get her day started in a happy way. She asked if he would be her "little boy hugger," and every day from that day forward she asked the boy for a hug. This teacher reported that the child's behavior showed substantial improvement. See Figure 2.1 for more ways to connect or reconnect with difficult students.

Another way to connect is to develop an interest inventory (see Figure 2.2) to learn about your students' preferences.

Do the two-minute intervention

This is one of the most powerful relationship-changing strategies I know. During two minutes each day for 10 consecutive days, find a way to develop a relationship with those kids who are driving you the craziest. Stay away from expressing anything critical during this time. It is a time to share information about yourself or ask questions to get to know the other person better. If the other person is reluctant to talk or rejecting, do not get discouraged. Make a commitment to keep at it every day for two weeks. Do this with only one person at a time. Most teachers report that initial reluctance and distance from students is gradually replaced with a smoother flow of communication often accompanied by better behavior.

> *Suggestion:* You can do the two minute intervention anywhere at school, but it is best to try to weave it into your lesson plans for several days. When you do, it makes you think about how you might use class time to connect with the targeted student. It is least time-consuming and intrusive to have your two minutes while your other students are engaged in an assignment or project that requires less of your direct teaching (i.e., students are reviewing material with each other or doing an assignment in their groups).

FIGURE 2.1

Easy ways to connect or reconnect with your difficult students

• *2 x 180.* If you teach high school, try to acknowledge each of your students for at least two seconds every day during the course of the 180-day school year. It can be as simple as smiling, saying hello, or commenting on something specific, such as, "I really like the effort you put into your paper."

• *Noticing.* Every day, complete the following sentence in a friendly way with at least five students you have the least contact with: "I noticed when you_____."

• *Write notes of appreciation.* Occasionally compile a brief thank-you note for showing effort.

• *Have a suggestion box.* Invite your students to offer ideas and suggestions about how the class can be improved. Read every suggestion and, if they sign their name, tell your students that you will either implement it or tell them why you won't/can't.

• *Show up at an event outside the classroom.* Attend a game or show up at a hang-out place at school to have informal contact with a student. You don't have to stay very long, but be sure to be seen by the student.

• *Keep pictures of your family or friends in the classroom.* This personalizes you, the teacher, and makes you more approachable.

• *Nicknames.* Develop a friendly nickname for each student (i.e., Wonderful Wanda; Jovial Jack; Fantastic Frank; Lively Lu).

• *The positive postcard.* Periodically send home postcards addressed either to students or their parents that briefly outline and praise specific positive behavior or achievement you have recently observed. I know a teacher who writes these notes for parents but first shows them to students. She tells them to tell her when they think she ought to send them home.

Note: Some of these strategies and many more can be found in *Connecting with Students* (ASCD, 2001).

FIGURE 2.2

Things about me

Please complete the following sentences:

- Something I like to do outside of school is _____.

- My favorite holiday is _____.

- People I like best _____.

- When I was little, I used to _____.

- When I get older, I hope to _____.

- I wish _____.

- During my free time, I prefer _____.

- A place I would like to visit is _____.

- I feel most important when _____.

- My best subject at school is _____.

- It is hard for me to_____.

- When I am by myself, I like to _____.

- With other people, I _____.

- My favorite video game is _____.

- My favorite movie is _____.

- It would be helpful for my parent/guardian to _____
_____.

- Some of my interests that I wish my teachers would ask
about are _____.

- I learn best when teachers _____.

- Not too many people know that I _____.

Do the 5 x 10

Consider spending five minutes a day with 10 students each month to see how they are doing and what, if anything, they think you can do to help make their school experience as positive as possible. Try to do this at least once with each of your students. You might need to modify the time frame. For example, if you are a secondary teacher with more than 100 students, you'll need to see a few more than 10 each month. You can also modify the time. Three things to say are:

- How are things going in class (or at school)?
- Is there anything I can do to help? If no is the answer, ask, "Are you sure?"
- Thanks for letting me know. If you think of anything else, please either see me or write to me.

Express appreciation every day to your most difficult students

Find something positive every day for two weeks about each of your difficult students and express that to them. It might be about something they did, something they wore, or something they said. It might be as simple as appreciating the effort they made to show up. If you can't think of something positive to say, at least act friendly with a smile and a welcoming attitude. You might even consider offering a compliment about a behavior that you often find troubling. This is known as reframing. For example, if a student challenges you, consider thinking of that student as strong-willed. Your compliment might go as follows:

> Bill, you are a strong-willed person with a mind of your own. Even though we sometimes get into it with each other, I have a lot of respect for how you stand up for what you think is right.

Most students will show increased cooperation when they feel accepted for who they are. John Seita, a colleague of mine and a well-respected youth services professional who was in and out of detention centers and foster care homes as a youth, advises us to help difficult youth develop a "fan club" of support. At the very least, we need to be in it. While we need to be a cheerleader for all of our students, it is especially necessary for our students who have the fewest fans.

Let your students be in charge of things you don't want to do

When you get a chance, make a list of all the things you have to do every day at work. The list should include an overview of the content you have to teach, as well as all the organizational stuff that goes along with it (i.e., collecting lunch money, dealing with visitors, passing out papers, collecting papers, overseeing supplies, cleaning the chalkboard, etc.). After the list is as comprehensive as it can be, put an asterisk next to those items that *only* you can do. The items should include those for which your students lack the skill because they just aren't old or mature enough, or those that required you to go to school long enough to get your teacher certification. For all the others, consider assigning them to your students, especially the ones that are driving you crazy. Often, the students that are the most difficult to handle are seeking a feeling of power and control. They need evidence that what they do influences others and the world around them. Their behavior often improves when they are given responsibility for the oversight of a valued task. I recall a student who was strongly suspected of stealing things. His teacher told him exactly where she kept her purse and gave him the responsibility of making sure that it and other items were kept safe. She took him aside and said, "Because some things have been disappearing, I want to make sure that there is another set of eyes looking out for my stuff and others. You're my guy. Keep your eyes open and let me know if you see anything suspicious!" This teacher took a fairly large risk (although she did keep virtually all valuables out of the purse after the stealing started), but reported that stealing in her class virtually disappeared.

Reason is usually better than reprimand

Reprimands are rarely useful with difficult students and adults. It is not enough to simply tell the person what you want. If you can't explain why the information is important or useful, expect the noncompliant kids to challenge you with their words or actions. They don't care about consequences, and they are unimpressed by the threat of failure or for that matter much of anything. Sensible explanation usually works far better. Most students will do what you ask if it makes sense. When they ask why they need to learn what you are teaching, let them know. How will it be of benefit to them? Are there any practical applications or examples that they can relate to? Beyond the obvious, have an answer for why you are teaching the content you do. Sometimes there may not be a good explanation. Give the best one you can, injecting some humor along the way if at all possible. I know a 4th grade teacher who answers why questions that lack a good reason in two ways. She says:

"First, it's going to be on the test and second, someday you might be a parent and you won't want to look stupid when your kid asks you to explain this and you don't know."

Begin requests with an assertive *please*

Usually what works in life works with kids. This is no exception. For starters, think of a student with whom you frequently battle. For a full day, concentrate on beginning each request for compliance by pairing the word *please* with the assertive body language and tone of voice described at the beginning of the chapter.

End requests for compliance with a *thank you*

It is remarkable that students are much more likely to do what we ask when we thank them for their cooperation before they give it. Some examples:

> "Jack, thanks for ignoring Bill's nasty comment. I appreciate it."
> "Sharika, I look forward to seeing you on time tomorrow. Thanks for making the effort."
> "Liz, you obviously feel that I am treating you unfairly. If you want to discuss this further, thanks for waiting until after class."

Use encouraging statements every day

Words of encouragement keep students connected and motivated. Below are 16 sentences that take little time to say. Make a habit of sharing at least one of these each day for 15 consecutive days to any student who is giving you a hard time.

- You really hung in there until you finished that assignment.
- That was really cool.
- Wow, you pushed yourself today, and it really worked out.
- I was so impressed today when you_____.
- That was awesome!
- That took some special effort.
- I hope you feel proud because you should.
- Thanks for putting a smile on my face.
- Not exactly what I thought but very interesting.
- It is not easy to_____, but you are making it happen.
- Your cooperation is really appreciated. Thanks.

- That was flat-out good!
- That was quite an accomplishment.
- Sweet!
- Congratulations (and then be specific about what you are congratulating).
- You are really getting to where you need to be. Keep it going!

Use incentives wisely

Much has been written about the pros and cons of using incentives to encourage better behavior. The bottom line with tough classes is that using tangible incentives can be an effective behavior management component. In general, you want students to know how they can earn rewards, but you want to be sure to keep an element of surprise in the mix. I like having auctions on a semi-regular basis, but like a good television show, you can't watch the same one over and over without getting bored. So, do variations on the theme. When students do the right thing, a slip of paper with their name gets put into a box with a drawing held periodically. If their name gets drawn, they win a reward of some type. This can usually be extra time doing a preferred activity or some small tangible reward.

Probably the most powerful way to influence behavior is to reward the class on behalf of an individual. In essence, the entire class celebrates one or a few students' academic or behavioral achievement. For example, Charles has done a much better job participating in a class activity without distraction, bothering somebody else, or getting out of his seat. Ms. Jones, his teacher, says privately to Charles, "You have been awesome today, Charles. You have stayed in your seat and gotten your work done." She then turns her attention to the class and says, "Listen up everybody. To celebrate some special accomplishments of Charles, today we all get five minutes at the end of class to enjoy a favorite activity. Keep up the good work, Charles." It is important to let your students know that you won't be doing this every day even though you could because of the time it takes, and that they aren't to ask for a celebration because only you will decide.

Helpers everyone?

Challenge your students to do something every day to help at least one other person in school and one person outside of school. Encourage your students to keep a helper's journal. Read them periodically and offer comments when appropriate. Examples of helping at school could include inviting a lonely student to eat lunch at your table, standing up to bullies by refusing to join them in picking on others or by telling an adult, reminding someone to follow the rules before he gets in trouble, and lending a pencil to someone who forgot her own. Encourage students to add others to the list. Outside of school, helping could be doing things like serving food to the homeless through your church, running an errand for a neighbor, or offering to help with a chore at home before being asked. There are many ways of networking your students outside of the classroom to encourage helping. A teacher in a large Midwestern city who works with emotionally disturbed students connected his students to the Make a Wish foundation. His students meet with sick children, and after hearing their wishes, fund-raising activities are planned to provide financial support. It is common for his students to meet with sick children, see them off on their trips, welcome them home, and hear how things went. This teacher has marveled at the substantial positive changes he has observed in his students and the strong sense of community they feel at having a shared purpose.

> *Suggestion:* There is research that suggests that a person's happiness can be increased simply by counting one's own acts of kindness for one week (Otake, Shimai, & Frederickson, 2006). Brainstorm with your class to come up with as many acts of kindness as they can think of. Then

challenge each student to write down every act of kindness they do for one week. At the end of the week, have
each student count the number of kindnesses performed.
Without making this a competition, have a discussion
asking students if they'd like to share some of the things
they did and how it made them feel.

A baker's dozen ways to set kids up for success

Many students who are sources of stress believe they are incapable
of success. To keep from feeling the pain of failure, they turn to
horseplay, refusal to work, and disruption. It is very much within
our interest to make it really hard for them to fail. Here are some
additional ways:

Three Rs (Redo-Retake-Revise). Allow students more than
one chance to do well on an assignment, project, or test. Let students know that the highest grade can only be earned the first time
for excellent performance (to discourage students from delaying
giving their best effort), but make it so that much better grades can
be achieved on subsequent efforts. For example, if a student redoes
an assignment and it would normally earn a 95 percent the first
time, he is graded down to a 90 percent the second time and 85
percent the third time. Some teachers are more comfortable having
a maximum ceiling for redone or even late work.

Give tests occasionally that are impossible to fail. Ask
open-ended or opinion questions occasionally on a test and be
sure to count the results fully. For example, "Who do you think
is a better rapper and why?" "What are two things you love about
where you live?" "What two things would you change to make your
neighborhood a better place?"

Use the blue light special. Consider some symbol that you
can occasionally use to identify a class period as "make-up" time.
I know a teacher who uses a flashing blue light that gives students
an opportunity to catch up on back assignments during that class

period. If students are not behind, they can earn extra credit for helping students who are.

Build exercise and music into your lesson. Music and exercise are excellent ways to vary your lessons and involve your students who learn better when traditional material is paired with these modalities. A few excellent resources are songsforteaching. com and *Classroom Activators: 64 Novel Ways to Energize Learners.*

Build on mistakes and partially correct answers. Try to focus the need for improvement on what was done relatively well. For example, "Phil, you got the first three steps right, but then you took a wrong turn, which is easy to do. Let me show you how that fourth step needs to get done." Follow this up by giving another problem requiring the same four steps.

Wild card. My son Brian invented this strategy. Allow students one or two wild-card questions on each test or assignment. The wild card is a substitute question and answer pertaining to the topic that is chosen by the student for one they don't know on the test.

Have kids occasionally grade themselves. Ask students to grade what they think they earned on assignments that leave room for judgment, such as an essay. If you believe they were overly generous in their grading, point out how you disagree, remind them of a rubric if you have one, or share an example of a product worthy of the grade sought by the student. End by offering the student the option of the three Rs above.

Get them to notice they already have what it takes. When students are successful, show or explain that they already have what it takes. Point out that all they need to do is use the skills they already have more often. For example, "Kim, look at this. You practiced these problems yesterday, and you did much better on the test. What do you think made the difference?" Another example: "I heard Dennis say some mean things to you, but you told him to stop, and when he didn't, you came and told me rather than hit him. That was awesome! How did you remember to stay out of trouble?"

Level with them but challenge them. Many anti-authority students respond to challenge. For example: "It's great to see you showing leadership by telling other kids to stop bugging Carlos. But anybody can be a leader for a day. The real test is to see if you are enough of a leader to show Carlos your friendship by inviting him to eat lunch with you and your buddies. I'm not so sure." Another example, "I am convinced that we cannot get through an entire class without someone telling somebody else to shut up. There is no possible way this class has it in you to prove me wrong. But just in case you do, no homework tonight. Not that I have to worry because there's no way." If they succeed, "So you didn't say shut up for one full period. Big deal! Okay you surprised me, but even a bunch of 4-year-olds could probably do it for one day. I doubt you could pull it off today and tomorrow. I guess we'll see."

Set limits around homework. Homework should be for review, practice, or application. Try to stay away from giving new material to be learned through homework. Homework should also never be for busywork or simply to meet a school or district mandate. Don't waste the students' time and tell them that you will not waste their time by giving them useless assignments. Make your homework assignments meaningful by offering fewer of them. But when you give an assignment, communicate to them that you expect it to be done well because it is important. Let them know that you will do your best to explain the importance of the assignment, but there may be times that they will simply have to trust your judgment. Finally, if any student thinks he will not benefit from doing the assignment you give, offer that student an opportunity to present an idea for a more meaningful assignment that will show you his understanding.

Homework as extra credit. I have seen more than a few students suffer needless failures for not doing assignments when they seem perfectly able to do well on more objective measures. If a student can get a 90 percent on a test without ever doing an assignment, perhaps the assignment was unnecessary for the student to do. Consider having students earn extra credit by doing assignments that can be used to improve rather than penalize performance.

Focus on today, not on the state test. Keep your kids motivated by focusing on what they will learn today rather than on how they will be judged at the end of the year. This is best accomplished by making clear to them that assignments, grades, and consequences will be based on the principle of helping each student get better each day than they were the day before. To the extent possible, determine grades, assignments, and consequences based upon comparing each student to his previous performance rather than some arbitrary standard (for more on the distinction between "fair" and "equal," see *Discipline with Dignity,* 3rd edition, 2009.).

Start class with an open book quiz. This is another strategy I learned from my son Brian, who had great success using it with many of his challenging students. Give a quiz during the first 5 to 10 minutes of class that provides a basic review of the lesson taught the day before. Allow your students to use their notes and text as they answer the questions. Be sure to tell them what you will ask the next day as you end class, and watch while students essentially write down the answers to the questions you plan to ask. This virtually always guarantees a 100 percent to students who are on time and have their notes/text. Even better, by copying their notes to answer the questions, they are gaining another means of practice.

Keep your focus on the outcome

Too often we wind up in power struggles with students over their noncompliance with something that is actually relatively unimportant in the scheme of things—like whether or not they did a homework assignment or accepted a consequence gracefully. Further, it is not uncommon for teachers to wind up with hard feelings toward administrators for not doing enough when students misbehave. In my view, a consequence or an assignment should be viewed as a vehicle that we travel in to get to a destination. Should it matter if someone did not do an assignment if they can demonstrate an understanding of the material? If a student does all the work but fails to master the material, of what good was his compliance? If a student is suspended for five days to show that we mean business but returns unchanged, did being tough accomplish the goal? Be firm when it comes to your expectations of outcome, but flexible about process. Many times, I will say to a student, "Riley, you are better than that. What consequence will best help remind you that teasing another student is unacceptable, because I will not stand for that?!" If Riley gives an unspecific answer or none at all and you think a phone call home could be effective, tell her, "I am inclined to call home and discuss this with your mom unless I hear something better from you. Let me know after class if that will be necessary."

Intervention Strategies

Arguing, engaging in power struggles, sending to the office, and giving up are the most common outcomes when students refuse to behave. Repeated exposure to students who act like they don't care or who make it difficult to teach can get even the best teachers to want to throw in the towel. When kids push your buttons despite all of your efforts at prevention, your goal should be to stop the behavior quickly so that you can get back to teaching while keeping the student in class. Referrals should be limited to behaviors that compromise safety or that make it impossible to teach. The strategies in this section show you how to stop misbehavior quickly and respectfully while making it difficult for students to continue to disrupt. This will give you more time to teach and will help you enjoy those students who can otherwise make teaching painful. Keeping students in class and then dealing with them later is best accomplished by letting all of your students know you won't be stopping class to handle each incident of inappropriate behavior, as discussed earlier in this chapter. With rare exception, it is best to give consequences or seek more long-term solutions to the problem after class when there is no audience around.

Don't take offensive behavior personally

When our buttons are pushed, it is natural to either fight or run. Yet neither are good options when we are spending 180-plus days with our students. Bruce Feiler (2010) wisely advises that when things aren't going your way with students, keep your cool, don't threaten, and give them an out. To remain in charge of yourself, it is important to neutralize otherwise offensive comments or gestures. For example, if instead of a student hurling an "f-bomb," which would normally make us angry, try to hear it as if you heard him say "computer" or "light bulb," which would make most of us pause incredulously and maybe even laugh. Try to place a buffer between your natural reaction and the provocation so that you can decide what you want to do without knee-jerk reacting. If flipped off, try to picture it as if the student flashed his pinky rather than the middle finger. The only way to effectively manage provocative moments is for you, the classroom leader, to stay calm before deciding what to do next. Once you do, there are often many other options that can much more effectively defuse a power struggle than fight or flight.

Translate behavior

In many instances, it will help you stay steady if you understand that most kids who challenge won't back down because if they do, they risk losing status in the eyes of their peers. So to maintain their dignity, they call us a name, roll their eyes, and end with something dismissive like, "Whatever." Try to *imagine* the same student saying this,

"Mr./Mrs. (Your Name), I know you are only trying to get me to do the right thing. And I appreciate that you care about me even though I would never really tell you that. But telling me to do stuff in front of my buddies isn't cool. If it looks like I'm listening to you, they're gonna think I'm a wuss, and I can't have that. I gotta ride the bus with them and live in the same neighborhood. So when I shrug my shoulders and say, 'Whatever,' it's nothing personal. But if today you could cut me a break and do one or both things that you tell us to do when we students bug each other (ignore and walk away) I would appreciate it."

Things to say or do once you calm yourself down

After you have taken good emotional care of yourself by calming down before reacting and translating behavior, you must decide how to respond to a student's provocation. Conventional strategies include giving a consequence like a reminder, warning, detention, sending to the office, and calling home, among others. You might want to do one or more of these although rarely do these strategies work with your tougher kids. Threats and punishments often make tough kids feel like they won because they realize they have the power to get you frustrated. Further, none of these strategies can be used by students who may be in a similar situation at some point outside of class, so they don't get a chance to see an important adult model how to handle conflict. Finally, kicking a student out allows him to throw his education away for that day and, even worse, is often viewed as a reward by the student. All of that said, there are times to go the conventional route with a tough student. If it is simply impossible to continue teaching by having the student remain, then it is unfair to you and to all other students for the offending student to stay. You might also decide to show other students that the behavior displayed was so inappropriate that it cannot be tolerated in a classroom. This is a matter of judgment. It often works best to defuse the moment so that you can get back to teaching quickly and then handle the situation later.

Four-steps-or-fewer intervention

With most students, a simple reminder to behave is enough. But when that doesn't work, defusing can usually be accomplished with the four-steps-or-fewer process shown in Figure 2.3. Your goal is to get back to teaching immediately after the comment or action illustrated.

FIGURE 2.3

Four-steps-or-fewer intervention

1. Listen: "Ethan, you think I'm picking on you, and that makes you angry. I'll respect that."

2. Acknowledge: "Ethan, you are telling me that you are not planning to do what I just asked. If you have more to say, please see me later. Thanks for letting me know."

3. Agree: "Ethan, you are right. I cannot make you do things. Only you have the power to make yourself do the right thing, and I hope you will."

4. Defer: "Ethan, right now we are not on the same page, and if we keep this up, we are going to get into an argument. Neither of us wants to lose and look bad in front of everyone else. So if you want to talk more about this, see me after class. Thanks for waiting."

Remember, it is critical that you get back to teaching immediately after each of these comments and that you let all of your students know that you will deal with rule violators later in private rather than interrupting class.

Create cognitive dissonance when the "four-steps-or-fewer" isn't enough

While in most instances, the four-step (at most) process works well, there are times when it won't. At these times, the idea is to create cognitive dissonance so that you can stop a problem behavior quickly and get back to teaching. When a student is anticipating a response from you based on what she knows and believes about you, and you say or do something unexpected, the volatile situation often is defused. It is as if you blow the student's circuits and create a temporary power outage. This is cognitive dissonance. To make this happen, you must refuse to do what other adults predictably do. Excellent tools include smiling, using humor, laughing, agreeing with the putdown, and whispering.

The examples that follow were all shared by teachers at seminars. In each example, the teacher indicated that the response stopped the problem immediately and in some cases long-term. After you read these examples, realize that to use similar methods, you will need to change your mind-set and then practice a response to make this work for you:

1. *Student:* I really hate you!
   Teacher: Well, that's okay because I'm not here to be liked. I'm here to teach you science.
2. *Student:* I wish you would drop dead!
   Teacher: I will eventually, but your homework still won't be done, and that's the problem we need to solve right now.
3. *Student:* You are such a bitch!
   Teacher: You are right. And it would be in your best interest to remember that.
4. *Student:* You are a f*****g gay bitch!
   Teacher: Wow, I thought I had it all figured out, but now my whole sexual identity is in question.

5. Students are talking during class while another student or the teacher is speaking.

> *Teacher:* I am so sorry for interrupting you. I thought I was the only one speaking, and I was trying to explain something to the class. I did not mean to be so rude and obnoxious. Forgive me. Are you finished?
>
> *Student(s):* Yes.
>
> *Teacher:* Are you sure?

6. When inappropriate behavior is happening:

> *Teacher:* Do you have a problem you want me to solve for you?

7. A student with very poor social skills who was always trying to get his teacher's attention and that of his classmates said:

> *Student:* (Loudly) What would you do if I took off my pants right now?
>
> *Teacher:* I know you have more sense than that, but if you did, I'd probably tell you to hurry up because we have a lot to cover in this lesson.

8. A student who frequently interrupted and sought attention was dealt with in this way:

> *Teacher:* You know, I don't know why it is, but you are constantly needing my attention in this class. So I am going to give you all the attention you need after school today and for as many days as necessary.

9. During the middle of teaching a health lesson, Joe decides he doesn't want to listen. Instead, he chooses to draw. When redirected about putting his things away, he responds,

> *Student:* "Suck my_____, bitch!"
>
> *Teacher:* My first response was to become angry and personalize his comment, but I didn't want the rest of the class to jump on the bandwagon, so I said, "No thanks. Anyway, we're talking about the basic food groups, not human anatomy. That comes later in the text."

Instead of telling and demanding, try asking and listening

When you see students disengaged from learning, fight the temptation to assert your authority by nagging or threatening and instead see their lack of interest as an opportunity to get to know them better. Some kids will simply not learn unless what is asked of them makes sense. And in order to help someone see how it makes sense, you need to understand how that person currently sees the world. Watch what they do. Learn how they think. Try to find out what interests them. Say something like,

"Rhonda, it looks like you try hard to not do the work that is assigned. Can you help me understand why that is? What do you really want to do and where do you want to go?"

If that is too open-ended for the student, share a hunch and then listen to what she says and see how you might be able to incorporate her interests into your lessons. You might say,

"Rhonda, most students who won't do their work are either feeling like they can't be successful if they did it and they don't want to look stupid or they have found a way to feel in charge. But either way, it is important for me to understand what is going on for you. Can you help me understand why you don't work or maybe even better what other type of assignment you would do that could help us both know that you know the material?"

This might lead to Rhonda doing an art or video project on the subject instead of writing. At the least, if you consistently convey that you care more about who she is and less about what she does, she is likely to begin to trust you and eventually become more productive. It is important to fight the feeling that you must teach a lesson every single second. Sometimes a little personal contact can go a long way toward getting a student sufficiently comfortable to learn.

Suggestion: Try going for an hour by asking your students questions rather than telling them what you want. If you want Haley to stop talking to her friend and look at you, ask, "Haley, where should your eyes be and what should your mouth be doing right now?" rather than, "Haley, turn around and stop talking." If a student asks, "Is there going to be homework tonight?" answer "Is there usually homework on Tuesday night?" If you are challenged with, "What are you going to do if I don't come on time?" answer "What do you think should happen if you keep coming late? Tell me later." If necessary, you can always answer directly. But answering a question with a question shows your students that you respect their ability to think and make decisions, which is a valuable way to teach responsibility.

Put it on you

Frequently, we think that if only others changed their ways, our lives would be so much better. For example, if only my students cared about their work, teaching would be great. If only I got more support from the administration, things would be so much better. Although there are ways to promote change in others, try doing the following for two to three weeks.

Instead of saying or thinking, "Things would be fine between _____ and me if only he/she would (did)_____," say, "Things would be fine between_____ and me if only I would (did)_____."

Make the problem your problem and then invite your tough student to assist you in solving your problem. Many students will engage when they feel they aren't being blamed for creating the problem. For example,

> Mark, I know I hassle you a lot about not doing your work, and I'll probably keep doing that. I have too much respect to accept anything less than your best effort. You have a lot of ability, but even champions need practice. Most students who don't work are either afraid of failing, so they don't try, or they want to feel in charge. Either way, I hope

as you get to know me, you'll feel brave enough to take a
risk and try. But Mark, the real problem for me is I want
to be a good teacher for you, and when you don't do your
work, it makes it impossible for me to know if I am doing
right by you. So for example, today there are six problems
that need to get done, and by the end of the period, I want
to see all six, but I can probably live with either the first
three or the last three. That is the least I can expect that
will tell me if I am getting through to you. Which three can
I count on—the first three or the last three?

Apologize for your contribution

You are much more apt to get a student to look inside and explore
how to change when you begin with an apology for how you
might have contributed to the problem. The same is true when
there are conflicts with colleagues. For example, because most
students are very sensitive to what their friends think, when they
are corrected in class, they usually feel embarrassed. Many times,
their oppositional behavior or emotional withdrawal is a reflection
of feeling angry. You might start a problem-solving meeting in the
following way:

> Thanh, I want to start by telling you that I am sorry for
> saying stuff to you in front of your friends. I should have
> found a better time and place to let you know that I
> wasn't pleased with your behavior, and I will try hard to
> not do that again. In the future, I'll try to wait until after
> class to let you know.

After you say this, ask,

> Now that you know what I can do better, is there anything
> you think you could have done differently?

If the incident happens in a spot like the hallway or cafeteria with a
student you otherwise rarely if ever see, find a way to get with that

student after the fact to look at how to avoid a continuation of the problem and use the strategy of apologizing for your behavior.

What to do when students deny

When students say or do mean things, get caught, are confronted, and then deny what they did, they are usually trying to avoid consequences. At the very least, they are aware that what they did was wrong enough to warrant consequences. Often, they are also feeling ashamed to admit responsibility. Getting them to pay attention to their shame is often more effective in changing their behavior than whatever consequence may be appropriate. When you sense or know that a student is not owning up, consider saying the following:

> You are probably denying what you said (did) because you are better than that and you don't want to face stuff that is really below you. It's tough to face things you may have said (done) in a moment of anger because you are better than that and you know it. Everyone makes mistakes. The real challenge is learning from them and fixing them. So let's look at what else you could say (do) if you ever feel like that again.

Framing things this way will usually make students less defensive about accepting responsibility and more likely to accept or even suggest a reasonable consequence. You might conclude,

> So can I count on this not happening again or do you think there is some other consequence that will help you remember?

If the student thinks nothing more is necessary, either move on or say,

> That's okay with me, and I'm sure you're right, but just in case it does happen again, let's talk right now about what might be a fair consequence.

Because tough students often repeat the same behaviors, it is good practice to involve them in identifying probable consequences before the next incident.

Strike a bargain

Perhaps you can get more of what you are looking for but not everything you want if you look to legitimize misbehavior you cannot stop. This can often be accomplished through negotiation. Think of a disruptive problem that happens excessively but is not dangerous. Possibilities include getting out of seat, blurting out, complaining about things, coming late, and interrupting. Consider how you might feel if the behavior happened half as often as it does now. Wouldn't that be an improvement? It wouldn't be perfect, but it would be a lot better, right? Get with an offending student and say something like this:

> Max, you know how a lot of times we bug each other. You say stuff, then I get on your case, then you say more stuff, and we keep it up. Here's the thing, I can't live with you saying stuff whenever you want without raising your hand first because I've got to listen to other kids too sometimes. But I can understand that it can be tough to wait when you really have something you want to say. So how many times do you think you'll need to call out without permission today, because if we can come up with the right number, maybe that can work for both of us?

Depending upon what the student says, negotiate up or down. For example, if the student gives an absurdly high number (i.e., "at least 50"), say,

> No way would that work for me. We'd keep getting into the same old hassle. Hard as it would be, I think I might be able to live with five, but no more than that. Give me a number between one and five that would be tough for you to keep to but you probably could if you really worked at it.

If the student says, "Five," ask, "Do you think it would work best for you to say stuff at the beginning or end of class?" If this choice (beginning or end of class) would not be acceptable, offer another that you could live with. Finally, discuss possible consequences in case the agreement doesn't work on a given day.

> I'm glad we have an agreement, but if just in case you go over your five, what do you think would be a fair consequence? Just in case, let's figure this out now so that we don't need to bug each other later.

It is at first very uncomfortable for most teachers to "encourage" misbehavior, fearing that by doing so the problem will only get worse. Like intentionally walking a batter in baseball, realize that sometimes you have to risk making the problem worse in order to have the situation improve. However, the risk is very low because this type of strategy is to be used with students who already show a very high rate of inappropriate behavior.

Put the student in charge of his problem

Many students respond well when they are put in charge of solving the problem they created. An example of this strategy in practice was shared by a high school Spanish teacher. She designated the "loudest whiner" in one of her classes as "class complainer." The student was empowered to receive everybody else's complaints and to speak for the whole class during a time set aside by the teacher. This gave that student a structured time to share his concerns along with any other concerns expressed by other students. When other students complained, she ended it quickly by telling them to tell Felipe after class, and he would let her know. Most students who complain (or for that matter do many other disruptive behaviors) are often seeking either attention or power. These needs can sometimes be redirected by empowering the problem student in this way.

Enforce stupid rules but don't own them

Have you ever been at a loss to give a valid answer to a student who says, "This rule is really stupid. Why do we have to follow it?" If the best answer you can give when a student challenges the rule is something like, "Because I said so," or "Because it is school policy," those rules are at the greatest risk of being broken. Kids hate having to follow rules that seem arbitrary and make no sense, while teachers often feel stressed trying to enforce these rules. Many students think that we have much more power than we do. They don't realize that teachers are generally at the bottom of the pecking order when it comes to setting school policy. They don't see the bureaucrats at the state education department or the district administrators or the school board members who are often responsible for the creation of the rule. So rather than get locked into power struggles trying to enforce rules that seem designed to complicate everybody's life, advocate within your school for a change in policy, but until that happens, enforce the rules but distance yourself from them.

For years, I struggled with hat rules in schools where I taught, especially when there was no good reason. For example, gangs may represent through their hats, which is a good reason for the rule, but I worked at some schools where this was not an issue. I stopped the hassle at one point when one of my students gave me a well-considered argument. After asking him to remove his hat, Luis said, "But that's a stupid rule, Mr. Mendler. I actually learn better when I keep my hat on." When I asked him to explain, he answered, "The way I see it, when I keep my hat on, it keeps my brain warm, and because probably more oxygen goes to my warm brain, I can think better." Not being a scientist, I recall being impressed at what at least sounded like a clever excuse, and I let him know. I remember saying back something like, "Wow, I hadn't thought about that, and you might be right. But my problem is if you don't take the hat off and some administrator comes into the class, then I get into trouble, and I don't need the hassle. So thanks for taking it off." Continuing the battle, Luis said, "But it's a stupid rule." I looked right at him, and I said, "Luis, I don't disagree. Here's the thing. Because you feel strongly about this, I think you should work to change the rule. That rule was made by the school board, and they meet on Tuesday at 7:30 where everybody, including students, is welcome to voice their opinion to try and make things better. I promise you this: If you can get them to drop the rule, I will never hassle you about it again. I promise. Catch me after class, and I'll give you more details if you're interested."

Work to change rules that you think are stupid while enforcing them but create some distance between you and the rule. Kids are much less likely to persist when they get a sense that an important adult sees things from their perspective and gives them options other than to argue or disobey.

There are times you must temporarily overlook

Enforcing rules with which you disagree is important. Otherwise, students learn that the only rules they have to follow are those the teacher agrees with. Schools cannot run efficiently if each teacher is deciding which rules to enforce and which ones to ignore. Just like all players need to work together to give a team the best chance of winning, so too does each staff member need to make sacrifices for the good of the school. However, some students battle with us about everything, challenging every word, assignment, and rule. With such a student, or group of students, trying to enforce every rule is a recipe for nonstop power struggles, in which unfortunately some students are only too happy to engage. So as a practical matter, when you are facing tough students who can make life difficult, pick your battles wisely.

> *Suggestion:* Take a look at all the rules you are expected to enforce. Of those, put an asterisk next to those that you consider essential to making your class run as smoothly as possible so that good teaching and learning can occur.

These are the ones you should consider essential and therefore nonnegotiable. Stay firm with these. With the others,
try to find ways to soft pedal around them. For example,
you might relax the hat rule in the classroom, but make it
clear that they are to remove their hats whenever they leave.

Deepen your relationship with a suspended student

There is no question that students sometimes need to be suspended, but rarely does suspension alone teach the kind of lesson
that leads to better behavior. Rarely will you be inclined to reach
out to a student who drove you or others crazy enough to get
suspended. It is pretty much a guarantee that nobody else will be
reaching out to this student either. Precisely for these reasons, you
will blow a student's mind if you reach out during this tumultu-
ous time, and virtually always will you dramatically increase your
influence when the student returns. Remember, all suspended
students come back eventually, and when they do, you will want to
see better behavior. In his book, *The Taming of the Crew* (2009), my
son and colleague Brian Mendler advises teachers to call home and
have a conversation with the student that goes something like this:

> *Teacher:* Hi Dan. This is Mr. Jones. I heard you were sus-
> pended for a few days because of what happened in class.
> I just want to tell you that I'm sorry it happened, and I
> will miss you while you are gone.
>
> *Student:* Yeah, well I didn't even do nothing to...
>
> *Teacher (interrupting):* You know, Dan, I wish I had time
> to hear the whole story right now, but unfortunately I
> just don't. I do want you to know that I look forward
> to seeing you when you come back. I have no doubt we
> can figure things out so that this doesn't have to happen.
> I hate when you are suspended. One last thing: I know
> you rarely get work done when gone, but if you change
> your mind and decide not to fall further behind, I can

bring some assignments for you to work on. If not, that's
okay as well. By the way, if you start thinking about doing
something that might get you into more trouble, feel free
to call me first. I am always willing to listen. Please try to
stay out of trouble. See you in a few days.

It is wise to follow up this conversation by calling or sending
an e-mail a few more times. Look at follow-up as an opportunity to
revisit the issue that might lead to a better solution.

Invest in your opinion makers

Kids feeding off each other is what drives lots of teachers crazy.
When this happens, it is usually best to get together with the leaders at a time when the rest of the class is not around and brainstorm solutions with them. If you can get them to change, others
usually follow. If they seem uncooperative, let them know what
you plan to do in the absence of their involvement. If there is no
more leverage you have than what you have already used, that may
be as simple as telling them that you will continue to nag and hassle them as you have unless they can find a better way. For example,

I want to speak to you guys about lots of students calling
out, socializing, and otherwise not paying attention in
class. We need to solve this problem, because if we don't,
we won't be able to learn what we need to know for most
students to pass the test. I will not let you down. So how
are we going to fix the problem?

If they protest for being singled out, tell them that because
they are the leaders, there is no doubt in your mind that what
works for them would work for the others. If they come up with
one or more solutions that make sense, but too much of the
responsibility is on you (e.g., "Just call home or give us a detention"), seek consequences from them and for them in case what
they propose doesn't work. (For example, "That sounds good.
But just in case a mother doesn't answer or the detention doesn't

work, because so far it hasn't, what do you think would be a fair consequence?") Finally, seek their involvement in the enforcement of the plan. For example, if they propose that you give a warning, tell them that you will make them your warning monitors so that when you give the signal to chill-out if things are starting to get out of hand, they will warn all of the students in their area. You might decide in advance what their area consists of. The clearer the plan and the more involved the students are in its creation and enforcement, the better is the likelihood that it will work.

Two strategies for when students are entirely unproductive

Students become unproductive for two reasons: They either believe that they are incapable and they don't want to look stupid or they have found a way to frustrate adults and that makes them feel in control.

When the issue is competence. If you think a student is not trying because she is afraid of failure, make it impossible for the student to fail. For example, after giving the homework assignment to everyone, approach the targeted student and tell her that if she can get all of the problems done that would be great, but make her responsible for just one of the problems. You would say something like:

> Josie, there are six problems due tomorrow, and if you can get them all done, that would be awesome. But I am counting on you to do number four. So make sure you do an especially good job on that one because tomorrow I am calling on you to answer that question.

In some cases, you might even give her the actual answer to the question before she leaves so that it becomes virtually impossible for her to look bad.

> Josie, after you do number four, check it against this answer to make sure yours is correct.

As the student arrives to class the next day, ask her if she has number four done. If she did it, great. If not, tell her that she still has 10 minutes to figure it out,

> Josie, number 4 is not done, and that is not okay. In 10 minutes I'm calling on you, and I want you to look good, so get busy writing this down.

Be sure to have these conversations quietly. Setting kids up for success is very effective when the issue is *competence*. When a student does not believe that she can be successful, it is common to give up or act out in response to the difficult subject.

When the issue is control, a different strategy is necessary. These students show more widespread refusal to do work as a means to assert their power. They are often mostly or entirely capable of being successful, but they carry anger, which expresses itself in a quiet, passive-aggressive way. When this is going on, a very effective yet extremely unconventional method is to suggest and even demand that the student do the direct opposite of what you really want. You will want to reserve the use of this strategy with students at the extreme. And be sure to clear this technique with your administrator and the student's parent(s) before using it because it can easily be interpreted as you giving up on the child rather than a diligent (if unconventional) effort to spark motivation.

So if the student *never* does homework, give him a homework assignment that requires him to do nothing. For example, after giving the assignment to the class, approach the student and say something like,

> Corey, tonight your assignment is to be yourself, and if that means not doing the assignment, then that is what I want you to do. Naturally, if you show up tomorrow, and it is not done, you will get a zero. But more important is that I respect what you think is right and that I stop asking you to do things that you are against. Have a nice night.

If Corey does what you ask (nothing), he is being compliant, and it is important that you respond to his compliance in a genuine way. For example,

> Thanks for doing what you were told. The same deal holds for tonight.

Power-seeking kids don't want to be compliant, and they will feel uncomfortable when you set things up this way. If the student does the actual homework assignment given to everyone, he is simply testing your limits, so don't get excited. Instead, *react to his defiance*. Express neutrality or even displeasure. For example,

> Corey, maybe you didn't understand that I gave you a choice to do the assignment last night, and today for the first time in a long time, you actually did what was expected of everyone else. I guess I'll have to read and grade it, and I will, but maybe you misunderstood. From now on, I want you to only do assignments that you think are worthy of your time because in no way do I want to disrespect what you think is right for you.

By giving students with an excessive need for control or power the authority to make the decision (which is theirs to make anyway), you remove the main reason for them not doing their work. In reality, you have changed nothing because students always have the final say about their own behavior. You must believe in the power of the method to implement it in an authentic way, and practicing can help get you there. Most teachers will need to practice doing this in advance because if you aren't genuine, it will come across in a sarcastic way. If you find while you are practicing that you can't respond genuinely, don't use this method. But by acknowledging the student's power to decide, you paradoxically wind up giving yourself greater influence over the student's decision making.

Be sure to continue to give real consequences for nonproductivity like a zero. Although most kids who collect zeroes aren't influenced by another zero, if other students start complaining and claim to want the same assignment, a zero is a deterrent for most. Give the same option to any student who complains about Corey. Simply say, "If you don't do your work, what are the consequences?" When the student answers, "A zero," agree with him and ask if that is what he wants.

⁇ Questions for Reflection

1. Why do you think many little kids who start school with enthusiasm end up bored or unmotivated? Make a list of the tips you learned or were reminded of to keep yourself and your students motivated.

2. As you were growing up, what were your strengths? What did you struggle with? What are your strengths right now? What are some of your struggles right now? There will undoubtedly be moments with your class or individuals within your class in which your personal strengths and struggles will connect to a lesson you are teaching or an issue facing an individual student or group. Many of us might want to forget our struggles, but sharing both these and our strengths makes us more real to our students and ultimately enables us to more effectively influence their behavior.

3. When one or more of the basic needs for connection (I belong), competence (I am successful), or control (I am able to influence others) is unmet, students are likely to become challenging. Think of your three most challenging students. For each, which of these basic needs do you think is unfulfilled? From the subsection on prevention, identify strategies that you can shape into a plan for each of these students to bring about change.

4. Think of a student who pushes your buttons. If your goals are to quickly get back to teaching, maintain the respect of the class, and keep the offending student present, develop a plan based on the intervention strategies that can meet these goals. What do you plan to do the next time this student misbehaves? What is your

back-up plan? Finally, which of the three basic needs do you think is driving the student's inappropriate behavior? Develop a plan of prevention you can implement at other times that might reduce the likelihood of these behaviors persisting (it may be the same or similar to those you developed in response to the previous question)?

5. Pick two strategies for each of the six pillars that you will do for three weeks with a targeted student, group, or class.

6. Spend a moment right now and think of your best behaved or highest-achieving student. How do you feel about this student and how do you act? When you think about this student, what adjectives come to mind? When you interact with this student, what comments come naturally? When this student makes a mistake, how do you usually react? When you see this student's parent or parents, what do you say? For one week, act toward your worst behaved or lowest performing student in the same way. No matter what he or she says or does, treat this child as if she has already achieved the same level of performance or behavior as your best behaved or best performing student. Bring the same degree of energy and pride. Don't be dissuaded by what the student actually says or does. See what happens.

Key Chapter Thoughts

- Make it a top goal to be a cheerleader for your students, particularly those students whose actions make others want to turn away from them.
- Let your students know that it will be very hard for them to fail your class if they follow three Ps: *prepare, plan,* and *practice.*
- Responsibility and safety are both promoted when students are invited to join in developing rules and consequences based upon the values you know are necessary in order for good learning and good teaching to occur.
- Enthusiasm is contagious, so be animated when you teach and have fun with your students and the curriculum.

- Don't be afraid to share your vulnerabilities, although do so with confidence and conviction. Your students need to see you as a leader they can count on and lean on.

- You are much more apt to get a student to look inside and explore how to change when you begin with an apology for how you might have contributed to the problem.

- The only way to effectively manage provocative moments is for you, the classroom leader, to stay calm before deciding what to do next.

For the Administrator

Let your teachers know that you value students achieving behavioral standards at least as much as academic standards. Let them know it is okay to spend instructional time teaching and practicing appropriate behavior. The report, *Are They Really Ready to Work* (Conference Board, the Partnership for 21st Century Skills, Corporate Voices for Working Families, & the Society for Human Resource Management, 2006), found that the four skills most desired by employers were *a good work ethic, an ability to collaborate with others, good oral communication skills,* and *ethics/social responsibility*. Interestingly, other than writing and reading English, there were no academic classes/courses that made the top 10, yet I am sure that if we asked educators to identify the skills they spend the most time teaching, most of those most valued by employers would be toward the bottom of the list. In no way does the report dismiss the importance of academic proficiency in job success. In general, employers view many prospective hires as underprepared. *Both* academic and social/behavioral competence seem necessary for job success in the 21st century.

On a daily basis, be there for your teachers in two ways:

First, let them know that if they refer a student to you, you will do your best to send them back a better behaved student. Try to let them know what you did and ask them how it went. If the incident was serious enough to warrant detention or in-school suspension, strongly encourage your teachers to hold the detention or visit the student at the in-school suspension site in an effort to address the problem more fully. Make yourself available to participate in a three-way problem-solving meeting at the teacher's request.

Second, offer your teachers a temporary time-out from a difficult student—a practice that is very much appreciated by most. At the very least, do not send a student back to class until at least 15 minutes have passed from the time you actually saw the student. If it is at all possible to actually accompany the student back to class, teachers are even more grateful. To save face, it is not unusual for unaccompanied students to look as if there was a gala celebration with you in the office when they get back to class. They're playing to their peers. This dynamic is often diminished when you walk back with the student. Seek feedback later from the teacher about how things went after the student returned. Discuss any further actions that either you or the teacher think are necessary. Encourage teachers to use each other for purposes of temporary time-outs as well, but remind them that when they send a student somewhere else, they run the risk of disempowering themselves. Perhaps even worse, a referred student succeeds in throwing away his education, which should be a source of dismay for all caring educators. Reinforce the idea that when misbehavior occurs (see Intervention Strategies), the main goals are to:

- Stop the problem quickly in the classroom and get back to teaching.
- Keep the offending student present if at all possible.
- Maintain authority.
- Respond in a dignified way.

These skills need to be taught and practiced. Excellent teachers are generally able to quickly integrate and use effective strategies, so they do not need to refer students for discipline very often. Therefore, when they do continue to refer, it is a good bet the problem is serious and is likely to require greater resources. In these cases, if it is decided that there is not a better program for the student somewhere else, work with the teacher to identify a plan she can use that might involve additional resources when needed. These might include an aide in the class, greater parent involvement, a modified school program, and hands-on support from you. You can be instrumental in starting a mentoring program at your school by inviting the Big Brothers/Big Sisters program, perhaps volunteers from local churches, and other community outreach groups to deepen their involvement with your school. Great teachers can't do it alone.

Be sure to get to know your challenging students at times other than when they get into trouble. This is likely to increase your influence with them. Like your teachers, you can use many of the prevention strategies in the chapter. Finally, make it a priority to tackle behavior and management issues at a school level. Develop a theme for each week based upon your school's policy and values. For example, identify verbal behaviors that show respect and ones that don't. Encourage your staff and students to come up with activities that promote the desired verbal behaviors and that eliminate the undesired ones. Have contests between and within classes to show improvement. There are numerous possibilities: Which classes can say the fewest "shut ups" to each other every day for a week? Emphasize improvement: Which classes can say "shut up" half as much as they did last week? Add a skill the next week: Which classes can say "shut up" the least and have the most students show up on time with all necessary materials? Brainstorm possible rewards with staff and students. I know some of this sounds "hokey," and if these examples wouldn't fit for your school, create your own way. Without an ongoing schoolwide effort and activities to support that effort, even your best teachers and students will too often drown in a tidal wave of negative behaviors.

....

CHAPTER THREE

Working Successfully with Unappreciative or Irritating Adults

I can live two months on a good compliment.

Mark Twain

Some teachers are unhappy not because of their work with students, but rather due to tension or uncertainty with other adults. For many teachers, very long periods of time can go by without receiving praise and appreciation for their work. Other sources of dissatisfaction expressed by a number of teachers are:

- Colleagues with whom they need to collaborate and who have different styles or philosophies
- Parents who complain and blame
- Administrators who are unsupportive

It can be disheartening to show up every day to a place where the challenges of figuring out what is best for the kids are dwarfed by the challenges of dealing with difficult adults. School climate is one of those things that is hard to quantify but very palpable when you are in a place every day. It is such an integral part of the daily experience, and it is largely determined by the leadership, your colleagues, and you. Do you and other teachers feel welcomed or ignored? Important or taken for granted? Respected or dismissed? Allowed to be creative or locked into doing it one way? In my interviews with teachers, it was not uncommon for many to report feeling unrecognized when they make good decisions, have innovative ideas, make valuable contributions at meetings, or persist in trying to reach difficult students and challenging parents. Nobody likes feeling unimportant and taken for granted. While that may appear obvious, it seems almost human nature to notice when things go either exceptionally well or horribly wrong and to pay little attention when things simply go right. Virtually nobody pays attention when they flip the switch and the light goes on, but everybody notices when the lights go out. In a crowded supermarket, parents respond rapidly to a child's tantrum but are far less likely to recognize compliance to a spoken request in a normal tone. At a sporting event, we might remember the great catch or the boneheaded error, but rarely do we recall the many routine plays that were made effortlessly. While it might look routine and effortless to us, the gifted athlete undoubtedly had to practice his craft endlessly to make it look that way.

Take a moment and think about how often you notice when things are smooth sailing. How often have *you* shared positive feedback with a colleague about how well her class lined up? When was the last time *you* thanked an administrator for her organizational effort on a day when things went smoothly or a parent who signed the permission slip and got it back to you on time? In contrast, many of us are quick to resent the administration on a chaotic day or notice the parents who haven't returned the permission slip. In our busy lives, it is easy for us to forget how important it is to give positive feedback. A recent and well-publicized study of college students found their desire for praise trumped their desire for sex, alcohol, and money (Bushman, Moeller, & Crocker, 2010).

You will find many tips throughout this section to help you interact more effectively with difficult adults. Although it is desirable for people who work together to get along well, the real issue is whether trying to get along with colleagues will change your outlook. Are you at a school now where it feels to you that few if any other adults seem to really care one way or another about you? Do you feel taken for granted? Are there some colleagues or parents who always seem to put up roadblocks to what you do, what you want to do, or to changes that you think would make your school a better place? If you are a great teacher and happy because of the fulfillment you derive from your interaction with your students, it may be that you have little need for support from others. However, most great teachers need a support network of colleagues and leaders. We will look at techniques you can use to defuse conflict and influence change in your difficult colleagues, parents, and administrators. This can make your life better and your school a better place for you and for your students. Finally, we all thrive when we receive genuine praise and appreciation. We will look at how you can get your fair share. Getting and giving positive feedback is the most powerful key in creating a school climate conducive to high achievement and happiness. You won't be able to influence everyone, but you may have more power than you think to make your school more of what you want it to be.

Getting Others to Change

People have reasons for everything they do. Although our motives may not always be easy to decipher (even to ourselves), with rare exception, we do not act blindly. Consciously or not, we set up goals in an attempt to get what we want. At the extremes are narcissists who use people to get what they want without any regard for how their behavior affects others, and altruists who selflessly seek to better the world for everyone else. The end result is that people act in their own best interest to achieve the goals that will improve their lives and make them feel fulfilled. While I don't know Bill Gates or Warren Buffet personally, I am sure the billions of dollars they donate to better the lives of others is done because their desire to make the world a better place or to be widely recognized for impacting major issues makes them feel good. How you vote in an election is determined by who you think will make things better for you. It may not sound fashionable, but "What's in it for me?" is probably the most powerful motivator there is. When you want to get people to change their views or actions, it is important to figure out what they value or need and how you think *their* lives will improve or benefit by doing it your way. Why should others listen to you? How will they get more of what they want and need by giving you more of what you want and need?

Recognize people

Most people need to be noticed or recognized, feel successful, experience pleasant sensation, and think of themselves as important. So if you want to influence somebody, try to put yourself in the other person's shoes, and from his perspective answer these questions: "If I do it your way, how will I be recognized or noticed more favorably? How will I gain in stature, admiration, or respect? How will my life become easier or more enjoyable? How will I be able to make more of a difference in what I think is important?"

Be patient

Understand that change takes time and is rarely accomplished right away. Patience and persistence are virtues when working with difficult kids or challenging adults. Getting people to change can sometimes feel like watching Chinese bamboo trees grow. They require five years of watering and care before they suddenly spurt. During the five years, virtually no growth is seen, yet remarkably, in the fifth year the tree grows 90 feet almost overnight! Throughout my career I have seen too many teachers give up on strategies too quickly out of frustration when change isn't seen right away or the person changes quickly but these changes aren't sustained. Unfortunately, the process of change is usually slow and incremental, involving small steps forward tempered by temporary paralysis or relapse. People tend to revisit old behaviors as they acquire new behaviors. With colleagues and parents, it is not uncommon to think you have convinced them only to then see them pull back later. Buyer's remorse kicks in. Don't give up easily if what you want is important to you. Many times you must plant the seed several times in the same spot before it grows.

Commit to change

When you develop a plan for change, commit to it. As a rule of thumb, try the new way of doing things at least five times or over a trial period of at least three weeks. If during this period you observe change for the better interspersed with the same old frustrating behaviors, that would be an indication that what you are doing is actually working! It is only when you see no change at all after five times or three weeks that it is advisable to go back to the drawing board and develop something else. For example, if your goal is to get the teacher next door to run a quieter classroom, ask or offer suggestions at least five times before seeking help from someone else. To avoid sounding repetitive, you might vary your words or tone of voice. The same guideline holds true when you are trying to get yourself to change. By the way, when you are trying to change something about yourself or you are doing something to help a student change, it can be helpful to ask a colleague to observe you or the student during some of these intervals to help you know how well things are working. I know students who initially demonstrate very high rates of unacceptable behavior and then make substantial improvement, only for the improvement to be missed by their teacher. In the heat of frustration, it is easy to miss or minimize the fact that a student's "blurting out" may have gone from 25 times a day to 10.

Plant the seed

Years ago, Freedman and Fraser (1966) found that "to get your foot in the door," making requests of people that asked for just a little bit of change was the best way to get them to develop a new mind-set before asking for something more substantial. In that experiment, a researcher posing as a volunteer went door to door in a neighborhood asking homeowners to allow a large, ugly Drive Carefully billboard to be set up on their front lawns. Eighty three percent refused. At the same time, with a matched group of homeowners, a different volunteer asked homeowners to accept and display a small three-inch-square sign that said, Be a Safe Driver. Nearly everyone accepted the sign. Later on, the first volunteer came to the second group of homeowners with the request to set up the same large, ugly sign that had been requested of the first group. More than half of the homeowners agreed. The small sign planted the seed for acceptance of the large sign. Covey (1989) found that readiness for change is usually promoted by asking for small things first. When seeking change, it is sometimes necessary to be satisfied with singles because home runs are a lot harder to hit.

Strategies for Getting the Appreciation You Need and Deserve

Keep things in perspective

When we get frustrated and feel overwhelmed, it becomes easy to accentuate the negative. A complaint from a difficult parent can become "all those unappreciative, enabling parents." Your tough sixth period class can make you forget the first five. A band of annoying colleagues can make you feel as if nobody sees it your way. When there is a problem, see it as a specific event rather than as a pattern. You might have a few challenging parents, students, and colleagues, but most of your parents, students, and colleagues are probably fine. You just don't hear from them very often. I am not suggesting that you bury your head in the sand. Sometimes there may be a problem that is part of a pattern or trend that requires your attention. If you hear several complaints or it seems that none of your colleagues want to hear what you think, it is wise to explore how you are coming across. Maybe you are not in the right place.

But too often, excellent teachers get discouraged when they get anything less than excellent feedback. As the excellent teacher you are or want to become, you are naturally a sensitive and caring person who is aware of and close to your feelings. When you feel deeply about things, it is difficult to not take criticism hard. When I give seminars to teachers or parents, the feedback is usually excellent, but virtually every time, there are one or two people who are displeased about something I said or did. Earlier in my career, I would beat myself up and obsess for long periods of time whenever I read a negative evaluation. However, I continue to read their comments and I have occasionally been able to use their feedback to make the seminar better. I never stop trying to please everyone because I want to hit a home run every time. But most of the time, there isn't much I can do differently, especially when a hundred other participants felt really good about their experience. Keep things in perspective. If it is only a few complaints, don't ignore the feedback or give up, but keep doing essentially what you have been doing and don't make yourself crazy. Let it sting a bit because the hurt can provide motivation to get better. Then let it go. We can only control the effort, diligence, and commitment we bring to the moment. We have much less control over the outcome. When Admiral Thad W. Allen of the U.S. Coast Guard, who was in charge of coordinating the cleanup of the 2010 oil spill in the Gulf of Mexico, was asked how he kept himself sane amid all the criticism and complaints, he said, "I am careful about who I rent space to in my head." Excellent advice!

Remember what is most important

After a seminar I gave to teachers at a suburban school district in the Midwest, a teacher at the seminar implored participants to thank a teacher who made a difference in their lives, and one of the teachers sent me a copy of a letter she wrote to Mr. S. It read:

> I hope you know that you were really good at disciplining with dignity. You always made me feel so good about myself. You were such an excellent teacher and principal. I constantly strive in my own classroom to be the teacher that you were to me. The special bike trips and the trips to the volleyball games really made me feel important at a time in my life when things weren't picture perfect at home. I'm sure that you have heard this many times before, but you really inspired me to be a teacher. I have been teaching for 14 years, and I can only hope that I have touched or will touch a student the way you have touched me. Thank you for being you!

Once in a while, we receive appreciation from a student or parent at the moment of gratitude, but more often we touch lives in ways we never really knew and probably never will. Just the other day I was with a former student that I had counseled years earlier. She had left home while still in high school after having been an abused child, and she essentially raised herself. Sadly, she had grown up thinking of herself as stupid until her high school chemistry teacher noticed a sparkle in her and refused to let her fail. He told her that she had better show up to school or he would come get her. She now has a master's degree and is teaching high school math to students with learning and behavior problems. Perhaps you will consider writing a letter of appreciation to an educator who inspired you and probably doesn't know.

Learn to gracefully blow your own horn

All people need recognition from others. If you aren't getting your fair share, the best way to get the recognition and notice you deserve is to make your successes more visible. Keep a track record of your and your students' accomplishments and look for opportunities to publicly praise your students in the presence of the staff from whom you are seeking recognition. For example, at a faculty meeting, you might ask for a few moments to share the names of students in your class who have made the most improvement since the last faculty meeting. Take an opportunity to thank other staff who may have been working with that student. Acknowledge colleagues who are making your life easier and/or more pleasant. Consider approaching your assistant principal to share a thank-you for helping Charlie, a behaviorally challenging student, who has been better recently. Even if you don't think the assistant principal had much to do with it, share an appreciation anyway. If you are a great teacher and you are getting little notice, I guarantee you that nobody else is getting much either. Let the old cliché "what goes around comes around" guide you in this regard. In addition, find humble ways to let others know what you are doing. At lunch with fellow teachers or when you are around your principal and aren't sure how to make small talk, let them know you supervised last night's school basketball game (i.e., "You know last night while supervising at the basketball game, it was pretty cool to be around the kids outside of class. I don't know that I'd want to spend lots of nights doing it, but it was way better than I thought.")

You are much more likely to get recognition when you are generous in giving it. Almost always if you make people look good, they will make you look good. Dale Carnegie once said that you can make more friends in two months by showing an interest in them than you can in two years by trying to get them to be interested in you. There is so much to appreciate that can make us and others feel good. Years ago in a school district north of New York City, Rick Curwin and I were invited to do a multiday staff training in Discipline with Dignity. The district had been on strike until a few weeks before, and emotions were still tense between some staff who had crossed the picket line and others who had not. After the first half-day of nothing but griping and endless "yes, buts" to everything we taught or someone shared, I interrupted the seminar. I told the group that there was a lot of resentment and tension in the room and that little if any of it belonged to the content of the training. I explained that we knew about the strike, which usually caused much stress that didn't just quickly go away and that while there were likely still resentments that lingered from it that needed to get dealt with, I wanted to know if there were any appreciations about anything they could share with each other. After a few moments of painful silence, people began to slowly share their appreciations. Whenever someone tried to sneak in a resentment, we redirected the discussion to "appreciations only." The mood eventually changed, enabling them to deal with the negative emotions caused by the strike in a more constructive way, against a positive backdrop of goodwill toward each other.

Keep a log of things other staff do that you think enriches school climate. Schedule some time every week to share specifics with these individuals and let them know how you and others benefit from their efforts. Try not to overdo this with any one or two people and be especially careful to not overdo this with those in positions of authority. You don't want to come across as fawning. Simultaneously, keep a log of your students' achievements. Were any other faculty members or the student's parents involved in the plan that is working? Make a point on a regular basis of praising and thanking others who have had a hand in the student's success. Err on the side of giving too much credit rather than too little.

Seek your own compliments

Most customer service centers do not hear from satisfied customers. We don't usually write a thank-you letter when our car, refrigerator, or stove works. Rarely do we think about acknowledging and thanking our doctor when he gives us the right medication. Almost never do we read a story in the newspaper about positive race relations. It seems that either due to human nature or conditioning, we are more apt to notice things when they go wrong. It often takes a conscious effort to notice when things are going well. Seek your own positive feedback. Give your students a homework assignment to tell you the two things you do that they like the most. At an open house, ask parents to write down at least one positive thing they have heard or seen from their child about the class. Ask a colleague to observe you teach and then share specific things he/she thinks you do really well and any suggestions they might have for how you might get even better. Teach your students to do this with each other.

In the original *Chicken Soup for the Soul*, there was a very touching piece submitted by a teacher, Helen Mrosla. I have read it to groups of teachers many times, and every time I do, my voice breaks up as I choke back tears. In the piece, Ms. Mrosla talks about a lively, semi-mischievous but good-natured student that she had in third grade and then again in middle school. The young man joined the military and died in action. Ms. Mrosla attended his funeral and then afterward attended a gathering for the mourners. His mother instantly recognized her and thanked her for the impact she had had on her son. The mother told her that when he was killed, they found a paper in his pocket that had been written when he was in her class. The assignment had been for each student in her middle school class to write at least one positive comment about every other student in the class. Ms. Mrosla then collected all the papers and gave each student the comments their classmates had written about them. This soldier was carrying his paper on the day he died. Overhearing the conversation was another former classmate of the fallen soldier who took out his wallet and unfolded an aged yellowed paper with all of the comments his classmates had written about him. He told Ms. Mrosla that any time he needs a boost, he just reaches into his wallet, pulls out his paper, and starts reading.

If you feel unappreciated, is it possible that you aren't as generous in your appreciations of others as you can be? Give before you get. Upon seeing someone in the halls who looks unfriendly, do you initiate the first hello? Are you someone who unexpectedly brings cookies for all to the faculty room from time to time? Consider writing occasional notes of appreciation to colleagues and administrators as well as to students when they do or say something that is thoughtful of others. You might suggest this to others at a faculty meeting as a way to improve school climate. Save the compliments that others have sent you or write down positive feedback others have given and save it. When you are feeling down, it can lift your spirits to read these comments.

5-4-3-2-1: Use the most important words

This is a strategy I learned from motivational speaker Zig Ziglar at a seminar I attended. The strategy was suggested for employers to get the best from their employees, but the applicability of using it with your students, parents, or each other will probably seem obvious. Make a habit of using these words in a variety of situations. Remember, if you give, you may be more likely to get!

The 5 Most Important Words: "You did a good job."
The 4 Most Important Words: "Can I help you?"
The 3 Most Important Words: "Would you please?"
The 2 Most Important Words: "Thank you."
The Most Important Word: "You."

Suggestion: Think of some of the good deeds you do as a teacher that go largely unnoticed. Make a habit of positively commenting to others when you see them doing something similar. When you are having a bad day, what kind of support is most helpful? At least twice a week for three weeks, consider giving the kind of support you would like to receive to a colleague, parent, or administrator. This is relatively easy to do with people you like, so the real challenge is to do it with someone you don't. You might have more influence than you think!

Make yourself visible

We all have our people preferences, but guard against becoming a member of a small clique. You will have very little influence over school matters if you aren't viewed as someone who is both respected and liked by all school factions. Make a point of sitting at different lunch tables. Find a reason to occasionally drift on over to the other hallway to chat with colleagues you rarely see otherwise. Once in a while, head on over to another department to see what is happening. If you overhear a frustrated colleague struggling with a parent, facing a deadline, or trying to find time to meet with a troubled student, volunteer to step up and offer assistance. Offer to teach her class while she meets with the students. See if you can help him meet the deadline. It is not your goal to be the school greeter or rescuer, but ultimately you are likely to get cooperation and support in roughly the same proportion as you give it.

Get the support you deserve and need from administrators

Teachers often cite poor administrative support as a major source of stress. You have the best chance of getting the support you need and deserve by knowing what administrators are looking for. Frame your requests by first asking yourself how what you want will benefit the administrator. The best agreements are agreements that are good for everybody. Most administrators want high test scores, orderly behavior, and few hassles from parents and higher-ups. They are looking to move up the ladder. Many actually lack real authority as they are subject to state guidelines, parent pressure, budgetary constraints, and school board whim. In effect, administrators often have little power and decision-making authority, yet they are usually ambitious people who want to feel in charge. Administrators who come across in a bossy way want credit for effective practices that are happening in their building. Most love praise and appreciation in large part because they get so little of it. When things are going well at school, be sure to attribute the success at least in part to the administrator's contribution. If things aren't going so well, try not blame your administrator. He or she is probably trying to meet competing demands. In fact, try to acknowledge some strength of your administrator even if you don't always agree. For example, "Mr. Jones, even though I don't agree with your view, I respect and appreciate how strongly you feel about this. I know we both have the best interests of our kids in our hearts." It is especially great to do this at a faculty meeting or, if you have the opportunity, when his superiors are present.

Whenever possible, present administrators with research-based facts. They usually love facts, figures, tables, and charts that they can present to their superiors. Even if they don't, you can be sure that the powers above them are going to want "proof" of your claims, especially if your request involves increased spending. Diplomatic types usually want to avoid conflict, so they will often give you what you are asking for if it doesn't complicate their lives. There are circumstances in which you may not get what you want even after framing your request in the best possible way with few obvious obstacles. If you get the runaround without a sensible explanation from an administrator who is usually dependable, you might have done something previously that irritated or annoyed him. If you sense this may be the case, you might try to gently probe. Say something like,

Mr. Henry, I need your help. Your reaction to my request suggests that I might have done something to lose your support, and if that's the case, I want to correct the problem. Can you help me understand how I can get the support I need from you to do the best possible job I can do for my kids?

Some administrators are micromanagers who need to get involved in every detail. Nowadays with programmed curricula often providing scripted instruction in the teacher manual, micromanagers may take exception if there is any variation. Rather than saying how you truly feel (e.g., "Ms. Lopez, you are a micromanager with an anal personality who is stifling any bit of creativity in the school!"), it is probably best to take a less direct and more diplomatic approach (e.g., "Ms. Lopez, I am concerned that you may have lost confidence in my ability to make important judgments"). When she asks what you mean, try to show how her micromanagement has led you to that conclusion.

Unfortunately, there are some administrators in leadership positions who seem afraid to do anything. They form committees to study issues and make recommendations that are rarely implemented, have lots of long faculty meetings that accomplish little, and are always focused on "shared decision making." These folks are averse to risk or just simply don't want to be bothered. If you ever really want or need their support for something out of the ordinary, they are very likely to block the request by blaming somebody else or some policy because they also don't want conflict with you. Help them see how your proposal is directly related to furthering the school's mission. Ask permission to try something for a limited time (e.g., two weeks or the next grading period) or with a specific population (e.g., that student, my second period class, just the kids below the 10th percentile) rather than leaving it open-ended.

These are the forces you must appeal to in order to give yourself the best chance at getting what you want. You need to ask how your request will make life better for the administrator. How can she feel in charge of the decision making? If your administrator doesn't like to be bothered, try to make it easy for her to say yes. After making your case, leave her with a written authorization for what you want that requires only her signature. Try to think about what your administrator considers to be important. What are his objectives? How will your suggestion further his goals or improve the school in the eyes of your administrator's boss?

As an example, let's say you want to do something different with discipline in your class, but your school has a policy that gets in the way. Your school has trained everyone, including you, in a green card, yellow card, red card procedure that is supposed to be implemented with all students. You have been using the system, but you notice that some of your students do not respond to it and you want to try something else. You are concerned about trying something outside the policy without first getting approval from the administrator. The administrator is not usually supportive of creative, outside-the-box strategies, but you know that he is fairly overwhelmed with the number of referrals he gets for discipline. The question for you now becomes, "Will your new system make discipline better so that you won't have to refer your kids as often as you currently are?" If you think it will or is at least worth a try, frame your request for approval around how your administrator's work load is likely to improve. You might say, "Ms. Smith, I'd like to try something a little different from the card system for two weeks, and I want to discuss that with you." Next, tell the administrator what you have in mind. When you finish explaining, say, "My guess is with a few of the kids I have this year, especially_____ (name the kids known to the administrator), doing it a little differently will lead to improvement. I'm even thinking and hoping that it won't be nearly as necessary to call on you for help as frequently as I have been. Can I count on your support for the next few weeks while we see if this works better with those kids?"

Making a case that includes a concrete benefit to the administrator during a trial period gives you a much greater chance of doing what you want with the support you need.

Finally, if you decide the time is ripe for you to apply for a different position within the school district or someplace else and you have doubts about what your administrator might say about you, consider writing your own letter of recommendation. After letting her know of your intentions, tell her you would like a letter from her. After she agrees, tell her that because you know she is extremely busy with a bunch of things, you would be happy to compose the letter and give it to her for her approval and signature. In addition to making it easy for her, this is the best way to accentuate your accomplishments and highlight your strengths.

Work with the union to get what you deserve

I have heard that a common source of resentment among great teachers is that everyone gets paid based upon seniority with no attention given to effort and job performance. To rise in pay grade, many excellent teachers feel that their only alternative is to leave the classroom for either administration or another occupation. This is unfortunate and unfair. Great teachers are a treasure and they deserve great pay. Most educators agree that a better balance between experience and excellence is needed in determining pay rates. While this is a thorny issue that so far lacks a clear solution, this difficulty should not remove a potentially important way to acknowledge and appreciate top-notch performance. Although I doubt there is one solution that will work for all school districts, some combination of objective measures like student academic performance and subjective measures like ability to inspire hope and positive contribution to school climate can be found. As a dues-paying member, realize that you have a voice in your union, and use it. You may be pleasantly surprised at the reaction of union representatives at your advocacy for creating a balance between years of experience and pay for performance. The union is trusted by most teachers, so it is in a unique position to lead the way in offering solutions. Because there is little long-term research on this subject, your creative ideas may be especially welcome.

Getting Along with Difficult Colleagues and Administrators

It takes confidence to deal on the spot with inappropriate behavior from peers and superiors. Everyone is entitled to an occasional "off" day, but when you are in regular contact with someone that is often sarcastic or downright mean, there is a good chance that it is because they are unhappy, depressed, frustrated, or angry. Not only is it necessary to preserve your self-respect, but difficult moments can show your students who may be present how to stand up for themselves while preserving their own dignity. Many conflicts that escalate between students and end in tragedy are preventable when students learn non–harmful ways of standing up for themselves without attacking others. Kids learn best when they see adults they respect using the skills we want them to learn.

Listen respectfully and intensely even when you disagree

Most of us have trouble listening to others share their thoughts completely, especially when we aren't agreeing with what we are hearing. The next time you are listening to someone with whom you disagree, refrain from offering your opinion until you have first actively listened and gotten affirmation from the speaker that you heard correctly. For example,

If I understand correctly, you are saying that you think students are too young to be involved in making rules, and it is the adults who should offer all the guidance and expect compliance. Am I hearing you correctly?

Resist the temptation to interrupt either by prematurely offering your opinion or by asking a question. Wait to speak until you are sure the speaker is finished. While waiting, convey your concentration by making eye contact and hold it about 70 to 80 percent of the time. This builds rapport. Lean toward the speaker and nod your understanding of their position occasionally, even if you disagree. Be attentive to body language. Watch the speaker's feet. If the shoes are pointed your way, it usually signals that the person is comfortable and feeling connected. When the shoes are pointed away, the speaker is more likely feeling distant. When you are talking, frequent blinking of the eyes from the listener is often an indicator that your message is not getting through.

Be specific when you give feedback

Be sure to tell people specifically what you want in a respectful way before assuming that they are insensitive to your needs or resistant to change. Tell an administrator what you need and why you need it. For example, "Thanks, Mr. Jones, for your help with Bob. You've probably noticed that I don't normally send you kids, so when I do, I'm usually just looking for a few minutes of time-out. Unless I ask otherwise, if you could just keep a referred student with you for 15 minutes and then send him back, I would really appreciate it." To a colleague who is abrupt with you, say, "You seem upset. Is there something I did or are there other things going on?"

> *Suggestion:* One of the first and best professional strategies I learned was active listening. Many others (myself included) have written about this, so I don't want to get into teaching about it in great detail here. Suffice to say that when you want to give feedback about something

that was said, it is wise to begin by reflecting back the most prominent thoughts or feelings you just heard. Then ask for any clarification that might be needed. A few examples: "You seem annoyed that I don't see things your way. Am I right about that?" "So when you didn't see me in the hall between classes, you thought I was shirking my responsibility. Is that how I came across?" After you hear an answer, conclude by giving your feedback without blame (e.g., "I can understand how you saw it that way. If I didn't know better, I would have thought so too. Just so you know, I wasn't there because I had to be with one of my students who was really distraught about his parents' recent divorce").

When you want to give feedback to another person, use I-messages. There are usually three parts:

1. When you (said or did) _____.
2. Tell how their behavior affected your ability to function

_____.

3. So what I (need, want, expect, would appreciate) is

_____.

Give a reason

You are much more apt to get people to do what you want them to do when you give a reason, even if it isn't very good, than you are if you give no reason at all (Langer, 1989). To informally test this, I asked fellow passengers at airports if I could cut in front of them on the security line by saying, "Excuse me, I have a flight to catch. May I get ahead of you?" I have found that about 60 percent say yes. But when I say, "Excuse me, I have a flight to catch because I'm in a rush. May I get ahead of you?" compliance goes up to about 90 percent. Just by adding the reason "because I'm in a rush" dramatically increases cooperation even though everybody on the security line is in a similar predicament. Incidentally, after doing this informal study, I stopped. I am not an advocate of using others to make your own life easier. But I will say that when I need someone to do something because the stakes are high, giving the best reason I can, even if it isn't very good, is generally better than giving no reason at all.

Give a reason that makes sense

You are even more likely to influence the behavior of colleagues, parents, and administrators with an explanation that makes sense. After all, you have little if any leverage with those people. Why do you want the parent or colleague to do it your way? For peers with forceful personalities who expect things to be done their way, agree with their opinion even if you disagree with their reason for what is causing the problem. For example, to a colleague who is resisting trying a strategy with one of your students, try saying something like,

> I know Daryl can be a major nuisance, and if I had him as much as you, I'm guessing I'd get just as annoyed with some of the things he does. In fact, sometimes I feel like I need to get away from him for a while. He can be a real handful, and I totally understand the desire to kick him out, especially in your setting. But every time he gets kicked out, he actually thinks he won. Believe it or not, this is what he wants, and I hate giving him what he wants when he behaves inappropriately. Wouldn't you agree? For whatever it is worth, I have found that when I go out of my way to spend a minute or two with him before class and give him a problem that I know he can do, I usually get better behavior. In fact, it works even better when I tell him that I am going to call on him for the answer. When he gets up and shares the right answer, his whole demeanor changes. Even though I know it would probably be harder to do this in your setting, I'm wondering if you would be willing to try it in your class for the next week and let me know how it goes?

Naturally, the actual words you use can be different, but they should reflect the importance of presenting a reasoned approach when you are seeking change.

Offer a meaningful apology

When you have had a falling out with someone, there might be something you did to contribute. I know the tendency is to blame the other person, and sometimes the other person really is a jerk with whom conflict was simply unavoidable. But if you look inside, you might find that there is something you could have done differently to avoid the problem. Perhaps it was the way you said something, what you said, how you said it, or how you reacted. Maybe the other person misread your intentions. Consider offering an apology nonetheless. The best apologies come with a plan that includes an analysis of what was done poorly and what you could have done differently. The words might sound something like, "I've done some soul searching, and I might have let you down. I think you were expecting me to give a more comprehensive overview on grade-level standards to parents at the meeting last night, and I don't think I got there. I feel bad about that. I have prepared a written document for your review that I'd like to send to the parents who were present that I think gives them more of the information they need. Please read it and let me know if you can you think of anything else I can do to make this right." If you are uneasy saying this, send the person a letter or note with the same message.

Choose how to hear the message

We can choose to hear and respond to any message of criticism in four ways:

- Hear blame and blame back.
- Hear blame, believe it, and blame yourself.

- Hear blame but listen to your own needs and feelings.
- Hear blame but listen to the other person's needs and feelings.

The first two choices are knee-jerk reactions that don't address what is really important. The first way produces the classic power struggle (e.g., Person 1: "That was a ridiculous idea." Person 2: "It's better than anything I've heard out of your mouth"). It is pretty easy to see that this is headed for an escalation of conflict. The second way produces self-blame and often leads to embarrassment or self-loathing (e.g., "Yeah, it is a ridiculous idea . . . I'll bet other people think I'm an idiot . . . I'd better keep my mouth shut").

The third choice is self-empathy, in which you listen to your own thoughts and feelings and offer a response that expresses where you are coming from. This is usually done most effectively in the form of an I-message ("I don't know if you meant anything by it, but I don't appreciate being talked to in that way"). The final choice is hearing what is behind the other person's message with the goal of conveying empathy. Active listening is usually the best method when conveying empathy. ("You must feel very strongly about this to speak to me in that way. What is going on?") When you are at the receiving end of somebody else's blame, criticism, frustration, or anger, and you want to steer the conversation toward a more helpful outcome, the last two choices are the best ways to stop an argument and make resolution more likely.

In a seminar I gave recently, one of the teachers shared that she uses an adult version of "red light–yellow light–green light," when somebody says or does something that makes her mad. I have been trying this lately and have been impressed with the results. A red light is most appropriate when you are quick to anger. Knowing you might say or do something you might later regret when in this state, stop and focus on calming yourself by deep breathing, counting, or taking a quick walk. The yellow light means you are still upset but a little calmer. In that state, think of explanations for the offending person's behavior that aren't personally directed at you (e.g., he's having a bad day; he doesn't feel well). Seeing other possible reasons for the person's behavior can further defuse your own anger and simultaneously promote empathy. A green light signifies that your emotions are composed and your thoughts are as clear as they are going to get. This is the time to take whatever action seems best because composed emotions and clear thinking make a good recipe for problem solving.

THINK

I have had the pleasure of working with Alex McBean, a teacher in Southern California who works with extremely difficult teenagers. Most of his kids are in gangs, and all have been either suspended long-term or expelled from regular school. Virtually all have serious anger management issues. He gains their respect in a variety of ways, including some that are conventional and others that are controversial and not easily replicable. It doesn't hurt that he is a powerfully built man who is 6'4". One of the skills he teaches his kids that helps them stay out of trouble is the acronym THINK. He teaches them to use this when dealing with people who are trying to intimidate or provoke them. I have found this behavioral acronym to be equally useful for anyone who is around somebody that says or does annoying things. Try it the next few times you are trapped around a person who is irritating:

Take a few deep breaths.
Hold your tongue.
Initiate positive conversation.
Nosiness gets you nowhere (so avoid gossip).
Know what to say or do to make the situation better or get out of there.

Go selectively deaf

Have you ever told your significant other what time you made dinner reservations, watched them nod, and then two minutes later they ask you what time you are going to dinner? Not that I am advising you to ignore your partner, but there are times when it is wise to selectively tune out. I know a teacher who says to students when she hears inappropriate language,

"I didn't hear that."

"I practice selective hearing."

"I know I won't be hearing that again."

With adults like colleagues and parents, it is probably best not to say that but instead to act it. The key is to hear the content that you might find objectionable but divorce the emotion from the content. You might need to respond to the content as if you are hearing about a new policy proposal from an administrator that you believe could interfere with your teaching or a complaint from a parent that might be legitimate but is delivered in an offensive way. When you feel your blood pressure rising, it is usually best to first take a few deep breaths while you imagine yourself listening to the calm of an ocean wave or the soothing sound of a favorite singer or instrument. With irritating adults, limit your exposure. Get away from them as soon as possible.

Try to make it a temporary lapse rather than a permanent quality

When you are in conflict with someone, try to see their annoying behavior as a temporary lapse rather than a permanent quality. You might say, "Ms. Samuels, I know that on your best day you would never say these kinds of things (and neither would I), so why don't we just table this for now, forget we had this conversation, and start fresh when we are both feeling better? I'll try to catch up with you tomorrow." Then walk away. Viewing someone as a good person having a bad day rather than a vengeful person with a foul mouth can work wonders. We all know there are some jerks working in our schools who aren't about to change. But as Goethe once said, "Treat a man as he appears to be and you make him worse. Treat a man as if he already were what he potentially could be, and you make him what he should be." Although I know this is not true for everyone, it is an attitude certainly worth several tries with difficult people.

Make the issue about an idea, not personality

When you need to work together with a colleague you don't like and who doesn't like you, both of you will need to put your animus aside for the good of the project. When things are stagnant or if you sense that she is sabotaging your efforts by spreading rumors or untruths about you, motivating her to be cooperative and truthful is best done by confronting reality head-on and then directing her attention toward something she wants. Try to make the issue about an idea rather than about a personality clash. You might say something like this:

> Mary, we have both been assigned to research the best math program for the district, and I have shared my favorable experiences with this program and the strong research that supports its effectiveness. I know you think that the emphasis on 'research-based' is overblown, and I don't disagree. But why do you oppose this so strongly? Is there another approach that both practical experience and research says works as well?

Reframe to turn the problem into an asset

When you are around an irritating person, try first to change your perception. Realize you have more control over how you view something than you do over what you are viewing. Nobody is 100 percent any trait. So no matter how unlikable a person may be, if you look hard enough, there will usually be some redeeming quality they have. There are exceptions. But you are much more likely to impress others and get both approval and appreciation from them when you show that you are impressed by them. When Ronald Reagan was running for president as the oldest candidate ever, he used age to his advantage by promising in a debate to never use his opponent's "youth and inexperience" as an issue. Reframing is a powerful tool that can strongly influence how we see ourselves and others. How we view an issue or person influences how we react to it. For example, consider these contrasting statements used to describe the same thing:

- Your face would stop a clock./When I looked at you, time stood still.
- You look like the end of a long hard winter./You look like the first breath of spring.
- She is very limited in what she can do./She can do a few things really well.
- He has a particularly hard time with math./He reads relatively well.

Are your challenging colleagues *oppositional* or *independent-minded?* Is an aide who takes no initiative *lazy* or *untroubled?* Is the principal who tells it like it is *loose-tongued* or *bold?* When we see aspects of the problem as an asset, we are less likely to be bothered by the problem because we can begin to understand the purpose it serves. More importantly, we have a better chance to influence change because it is easier to redirect one's strength than it is to fix a weakness.

Which do you think would work better?:

Example 1: "You need to take more initiative so that I don't always have to tell you that part of your job is to get the kids to settle down." Or "I admire how laid back you can be even in the midst of chaos. That is a great trait except when the kids need to settle down."

Example 2: "How dare you talk to me like that! Who do you think you are?" Or "I respect your strong views, which I think would make an even stronger impression if you just tone things down a bit."

Remember, people tend to resist change when they feel forced to let go of the familiar. There are times to tackle a problem head-on, but your path of least resistance is to appeal to the other person's best attributes.

> *Suggestion:* Turning problems into strengths isn't easy. It requires a conscious effort, so you will probably need to practice. For each of the following negative traits that would be troubling, identify a corresponding positive trait that reflects its strength (i.e., stubborn = strong-willed):
>
> *Hard-headed* = _____
> *Complainer* = _____
> *Rigid* = _____
> *Wishy-washy* = _____
> *Unresponsive* = _____
> *Lazy* = _____
> *Intimidating* = _____
> *Narrow-minded* = _____
>
> Imagine that an annoying colleague with whom you work is present. First, convert the annoyance to a strength (e.g., narrow-minded = focused). Next, offer a compliment on the strength. ("Kim, you are a very focused person, which at times can be really helpful, especially when kids lack direction. You are great at telling them what has to get done, and there are some kids who really need that.") Next, tell how the trait is a problem for you and what you want instead. ("But when Charlie is told what to do and not given choices, he goes ballistic, and then it takes me a

long time to settle him down. So when it comes to him, would it be better if you just left the discipline to me, or would you be willing to try offering a choice so that he doesn't feel like he's being backed into a corner?")

Now practice the process:

1. Identify the strength.
2. Begin the request by offering a compliment on the strength.
3. Tell how it is a problem for you and what you want.

Seek an opinion from someone who bothers you

Sometimes the most stubborn and uncooperative people will become much easier to deal with when you ask for their help or advice. Think of a colleague, administrator, parent, or student who comes across in an obnoxious way or as a know-it-all. Someone who is always giving his or her opinion or advice, especially when it is unwanted. Approach this person privately for help or advice about something that isn't really that urgent. For example, maybe you generally feel very good about the reading program you are using, but occasionally your students become bored. At faculty meetings, Mrs. Jones, the reading specialist, is always touting the benefits of another program as if it is the only worthwhile program around. She frowns when she has heard your support of the program you are using and has become unpleasant when you are around her. In private you might go to her and say,

> Thanks for your thoughts on the reading program. I am going to think about how I might be able to weave some of your ideas into the program I am currently using. I have found that a few of my weaker readers seem to get bored after about 15 minutes. Can you give me some ideas about how I might be better able to keep their attention when they begin to lose interest?

Everyone wants to feel important and appreciated, and most people love being asked for advice. Putting others down and constantly spouting an opinion are often done by people who feel irrelevant and powerless. As with difficult students, you might be better able to influence a difficult colleague when you seek their opinion. They are more likely to hear your ideas after you first seek theirs.

Take a moment right now and think of all the academic, behavioral, and social issues that exist in your class or school that affect you. Maybe there are certain rules or procedures that aren't going well. Maybe you have tried everything you know with a certain student or parent and haven't seen much improvement. Perhaps you are satisfied with the strategies you are using to teach the curriculum, but by sixth period you are bored hearing yourself say the same thing, and you are wondering if there is a different way to teach the same material. Perhaps there is too much noise outside in the hallways while you are trying to teach. Consider reaching out to a colleague who wouldn't normally be on your radar screen for advice and seek it. For example,

> Mrs. Lewis, can I have a minute of your time? . . . I'd like your opinion on something. I've got a kid in my class who I'm a little stumped by, and because your style is a little different from mine, I'm wondering if I can bounce some ideas off you to see how you might handle things. Would that be okay?

You might even ask Mrs. Lewis if you can visit her class to get a better sense of how she does things so that you can see if there is something you can learn that would apply to the problem you are facing. Although it can feel initially uncomfortable to ask, you might get assistance from an unlikely source. And even if you don't, there is nothing to lose when you have already tried everything you know. At worst, you will hear something else that won't work, but you'll be no worse off. Be sure to close the loop on the feedback you receive. If you did it and it worked, be sure to tell your colleague. If you decided not to do it or you did it and it didn't work, simply thank your colleague for the advice. If she specifically asks you if things are better and they aren't, you can give a noncommittal answer and change the subject, "We're getting there. Thanks for asking. How are things with you?"

When in doubt, reach out

How often do you wonder about what might be going on in the life of the kid who is always coming late or a colleague who usually seems bummed out? Are you curious how that parent you know who has five kids gets through the day? How many times do you pass a student or colleague in the hall that seems lonely or lost? Take the next step without waiting. Say hello and offer a friendly smile. Ask the next question even if it may take more time. I was recently at a school and told by two teachers at separate times about a boy who had been a very good student but had recently stopped doing his work and given up. He was convinced that because the world was going to end in a year (a contingent of people believe that 2012 will be the end), there was no longer any point in doing his work because there was no future. Both teachers shared that they had been unsuccessful in changing his view. Although both were concerned, neither had really engaged him with words like, "When did you start feeling this way?" "Sometimes when a person thinks the world is going to end, it is also their way of saying they are thinking about ending things. Do you ever have those kinds of thoughts?"

Some people feel that nobody really cares, so they withdraw into themselves and barely notice those around them. Glum people who spread their unhappiness weren't born that way. They often feel that unless they spread their misery, they might be ignored. While people are not likely to change quickly if at all, it costs you nothing to remind them that you care enough to notice them.

Sadly, many of us rarely pause to either smell the flowers or feel the raindrops. It takes a conscious effort for most of us to engage others who seem unhappy or preoccupied. We may be at a loss to know what to say or do. We may prefer to not get involved, fearing that if we do, it will take too much time and effort. So don't go beyond your capacity, but don't allow your limitations to prevent you from reaching out to the extent that you can. Ask how things are, and if the answer feels beyond your capability or comfort, share a thoughtful comment and direct the person to someone you think might be able to help. When in doubt, reach out. Be there!

> *Suggestion:* Try to get to know what makes the people that you struggle with tick. One of the best ways is to ask open-ended questions that cannot be answered with a simple yes or no. Here are some examples for colleagues:
>
> • In your experience, what have been some of the best decisions that have helped kids?
> • Who are some leaders you admire?
> • What signs do you look for in kids that tell you it is time to change the activity?
> • If you were in charge and could do three things to make this school better for kids (teachers, parents), what would they be?

Finding common ground

Getting to know an adversary better is critically important when trying to find common ground. After reaching out and getting to know a little bit more about this person, you might offer suggestions and ideas that could meet both of your needs. For example,

• It looks like while we might have a different strategy in mind, we both want kids to act more respectful.
• Here's how my idea about how _____ connects with your thoughts on _____.

- So if I hear you correctly, we both care deeply about

_____.

- It seems like doing (express a solution that is based on what you heard and what you want) could solve the problem. What do you think?

Know what to do with public displays of disrespect from peers

Although it is rare, I have seen instances in faculty meetings of colleagues attacking the integrity of fellow colleagues. More often, although thankfully infrequent, I have observed an administrator or fellow teacher engage in publicly scolding or correcting a teacher in the presence of her students. Such behavior is absolutely outrageous and must not go unaddressed. Public humiliation is never warranted. Consider the following steps should this happen to you.

- If a peer says something to you in an obnoxious tone or with words you do not appreciate in a public setting, try to defuse the situation right then and defer further discussion to a more appropriate time or setting. Your approach might be to say one of the following phrases:

  – "Now is not a good time for this. I'll be available after class. Thanks for waiting."
  – "I don't appreciate being talked to in a scolding way. If you have specific thoughts about what I might have done to offend you, please tell me when other people aren't present."
  – "There may be some truth to what you are saying, but the way you're saying it makes it hard for me to listen. Can we talk about this later when neither of us has to feel embarrassed?"
  – "You sound really angry, but now is not the best time for me to listen. Thanks for waiting until later when I'm not teaching."

– "That sounded disrespectful, but I'm sure that is not how you meant it. I know you have strong feelings about this issue, and third period would be a much better time for me to hear your concern."

• If an administrator corrects you when your class is there and it is the first time, see the administrator later and say something like, "Ms. Principal, should you need to correct me or share a difference of opinion with me in the future, I would really appreciate you waiting until my class isn't around." Should it happen again, firmly use one or more of the above phrases.

Addressing comments made behind your back

When the issue is about a colleague who is talking behind your back, what you do depends upon how much real power or influence that person has. Keep in mind that as weird as it might sound, most people who bad-mouth you actually respect you. If they didn't, they probably wouldn't give you a second thought. You are on their radar screen, and at some level you have some power that they would like. If the gossiper is widely dismissed by most others, it is probably best to ignore what is being said. However, if she has a strong following or you need to work with her on a project, it is probably best to indirectly and more tactfully deal with this person. Instead of saying how you really feel, (i.e., "Who do you think you are, talking about me behind my back?!"), which is likely to provoke denial and defensiveness, you might say, "I sense that you feel very differently about the issue than I do (then identify what you think are the differences), and because we need to work together on this, I'm hoping we can come to some common ground. Can you tell me how you see the situation?" Try to focus on the differences in ideas instead of arguing over personal issues. At this point, it is important for you to ask yourself two questions: What is driving this person's engine? How does what I think she wants affect what I want? For example, if you think this person is after power, see if you can find a way to show her how your position will empower her more. If you feel backstabbed with the other person trying to make herself look good at your expense, you might say, "I don't think you have the entire story. Is there a reason you left out the part about how I stayed after school to help supervise after-school homework for the last three nights?" If you think another person is looking for recognition, be sure to give her at least partial credit for coming up with ideas (even if she didn't) while you are sharing the results of your work. After your discussion, conclude with, "Incidentally, if you have an opinion in the future that differs from mine, I hope you will share it with me quickly and directly."

Keep away from toxic colleagues

It is best to not dwell on unwinnable conflicts and to keep as far away as you can from those who can't or won't be reached. In mythology, Sisyphus kept trying to push a boulder up a hill. Each time he nearly got it to the top, he would lose hold and the boulder would tumble back down. This went on endlessly. Some rocks either can't be moved or the effort it takes to move them is so extreme that exhaustion is the price. Realistically, you won't be able to reach everybody. If you find that your effort to improve things with certain people keeps failing, it is probably best to keep as far away from them as you can. Just as you want to learn from the best, try to stay away from the worst! Most faculties have at least a handful of teachers who are always negative about everything. They have become so cynical that they view virtually everything through a lens of pessimism. It is common for them to bad-mouth everyone except those who do things exactly as they expect. It would be bad enough if they kept their misery to themselves, but instead they are determined to spread their negativity as far and wide as they can. They are among the loudest in the staff lounge.

If you work for a rigid administrator who insists on everything being done his way or if there is a critical mass of negative teachers at your school, it is probably best to seek employment somewhere else. I have known some exceptionally talented creative teachers who are continually frustrated by obstacles put in their path. They are working in the wrong place. In the meantime, work at immunizing yourself from toxic influence. Be polite but avoid sharing any kind of news with them, especially good news. They have a way of raining on even the sunniest of days. I recall working at a school where a brave young teacher who became disgusted with all the negative talk about kids, parents, and administrators in the faculty room sat at a separate table and posted a sign that said, GOOD NEWS ONLY. Posted under the sign were "Rules for Sitting Here." Among the rules were: "You can say anything about anybody as long as it is positive; world, national, and local *good deeds* can be shared; griping and complaining are not allowed, but you can tell what you are thankful for." Before long, that table became one of the most popular among staff.

Realize that you are part of defining or redefining the school's climate. Influence it by refusing to participate in gossip, finger-pointing, and people-bashing. Either change the subject or leave the table in the faculty room if the negativity begins. Before you give up, consider being brave and challenging your colleagues. For example, "I don't know how dumping on Javon and his family is going to make anything better. Do you have any ideas about what *you* can do or we at school can do to make things better?" Put the focus on using words and practices that can make your school what you want it to be, but don't keep banging your head against an immovable object.

Getting Along with Challenging Parents

In a recent survey, nearly three out of four new teachers said that "too many parents treat school and teachers as adversaries." Thirty

percent of all teachers identified "involving parents and communicating with them" as the biggest challenges they face (*MetLife
Survey of the American Teacher*, 2004).

Seeing tough parents in a new light

Think about some of the more challenging parents who have
come your way. What kinds of things did they say or do that made
them difficult? What word or words best describe them? You
are probably not alone if words like "annoying," "bothersome,"
"meddling," "combative," "argumentative," "aggravating," "aggressive," "neglectful," "uninvolved," and "enabling" came to mind.
Probably few, if any, of the adjectives you identified were positive.
Now as hard as it might be, consider what *positive* words could
be used instead. Begin by exploring how these negative qualities
can benefit the kids. What happens when you substitute words
like "opinionated," "resolute," "strong-willed," "assertive," and
"determined"? Probably at worst the parents become misguided
or misinformed advocates who really care about their kids. Try
to see tough parents in this way. A middle school teacher in the
Southeast received the following note from a single parent who
had for months been argumentative [please note: names have
been changed]:

> Thanks for your help. I really do appreciate it very much
> even though I don't always tell you. Mr. S., I try so hard
> to keep my children on the right path, because trouble is
> so easy to get into and hard to get out of. Jamal's dad was
> never a positive role model in his life. When Jamal was
> younger, his dad spent more time in the streets, especially
> when he was joining a gang. Eventually, he started to lead
> a violent life, where he was abusive to me as well. He
> landed in prison for stabbing one person, and a couple
> months later, he shot someone, which landed him six
> years in prison. Once he got out, he and I never got back
> together. I let Jamal and his brother go to see him and

spend some time with him, but he bruised my oldest son, so I wouldn't let them go back to visit. Their dad was teaching Jamal and his brother that it was okay to be part of a gang. I refuse to let either of them to grow up in his footsteps. That is why I want the best for them. Their dad was only out half of a year, and then I got a phone call saying he was back in jail, this time for murder. This is why I am dedicated to helping my children live a life where they can make positive choices and not fall into the hands of the negative surroundings that we face in this world today.

Mr. S. could have responded by focusing on the many problems Jamal was continuing to have in his classroom. Instead, he seized the opportunity to bond with this mother by focusing on Jamal's strengths. Mr. S. wrote back:

Thank you for your e-mail. I, like you, am not giving up on Jamal either. His grades are so much better this year. He has been putting forth effort, and it makes a difference. I have talked with Jamal about his recent behavior issues. I told him I know he can do better and that I expect him to do better. Together we can keep him on track. I will keep you informed.

A baker's dozen ways to get and to keep parent support

While some parents are unfit, most are struggling to do the best they can for their kids. Rightly or wrongly, they may believe you don't care about their child, and they feel the need to stick up for someone they love. Many parents are struggling to raise their children in a complex world and are having limited influence. Some don't or can't value the importance of school because they are themselves uneducated, but they do care deeply about their kids. Try to hear their anger and hostility as a misguided form of advocacy. My suggestions are more likely to be greeted with appreciation when parents sense that teachers understand the challenges they face. Against this backdrop, you are likely to find the strategies that follow very helpful.

1. Initiate at least two positive feedback contacts about the student for every message of correction (e.g., phone calls, e-mail messages, notes).

2. Ask parents to identify three things their child likes to do; three things that help their child learn best; and three things they can tell you that can help you make school a successful place for their child.

3. Have a predictable time to be available (e.g., let parents know that barring special circumstances, all phone calls and e-mails received before 2:00 p.m. will be returned the same day and those received after 2:00 p.m. will be answered the next day).

4. Have a suggestion box that welcomes ideas from parents about how your class can be great for their child.

5. Make an occasional home visit when you want to share important information and you suspect that the parent will have difficulty coming to school (if you fear going alone, travel with a partner).

6. Send a holiday card to the family and a birthday card to your students.

7. When giving corrective feedback, start with the positive (i.e., "I'd like to start by saying that Jim stands up for himself, has a mind of his own, and works hard when he is interested. These are all very positive qualities that I think we can build on. What strengths do you see in him?")

8. When you speak to a parent, talk about "our" child. For example, "What do you think we can do to help Jen do even better? I look forward to helping our young lady in any way I can."

9. Express understanding of what parents are up against. For example, an informal survey of teenagers found that most expect to ask for what they want *nine* times before getting it. In view of this,

is it any wonder that many kids become persistent at whining, nagging, and complaining?

10. Always agree that there may be some basis for their concern (e.g., "There's probably some truth to Aiden saying that the class is boring. If you or he have ideas that could make it more interesting, I'd like to know. But I'm sure you agree that shouting out in class and refusing to work are not acceptable solutions.")

11. Appreciate all suggestions (e.g., "Thanks for that idea"). Then do one of three things: "I'm going to try that"; "Let me think about it and how I could make that work"; "Much as I wish I could, here's why I couldn't do that here."

12. Set limits firmly and respectfully when a parent crosses your line and says or does something you consider offensive (i.e., "Please don't talk to me that way.") If that doesn't work, terminate the conference, offering to reschedule when things calm down. Next time, you might try to have an administrator sit in with you.

13. Know and share a friendly greeting or more in the parents' native language. Naturally, if the parents don't speak English, you will need a translator to help communicate.

Guidelines for conducting successful conferences with challenging parents

Many teachers dread parent conferences, especially with parents who have challenging students. The following process can help, especially when the conference is designed to promote change. Some of the suggestions are similar to the ones above but are stated again so that you can see the entire approach:

• Lead with a strength before correcting. "Hi_____. Thanks for coming in. Before we get to what I (you) want to talk about, I've got to tell you that (student) can be a delight in class, especially when he participates in class discussion. He often has some very interesting ideas."

- Ask an inviting question. "Do you have any idea about why I asked you to come in today?" Or "What brings you here today?"
- State the problem. "When things don't go Pete's way, he can quickly get very upset and then he lashes out at his classmates and sometimes at me. What do you think is going on?" (Parent says, "I think he's bored. He says he hates school and that you pick on him.")
- Genuinely acknowledge concern by listening. "Wow, so what you're saying is you think Pete's real unhappy at school and not too pleased with me. Is that right?"
- Agree there may be some basis for concern but probe a little more. "There's probably some truth to what he says. In fact it is always my goal to be more interesting and have my students feel good about being here. If there are any ideas you can give me before you leave today I would appreciate it. Just out of curiosity, how is Pete at home when things don't go his way?" (Listen)
- Seek suggestions or problem solve. "Are there some ideas you can share that might help Pete feel more interested?" Or "Sounds like Pete struggles with his feelings both at school and at home. Would you like to seek some support from (recommend a resource)? I think that could really help."
- Conclude with a plan and follow-up. "Based upon our discussion today, I'm going to look for ways to give Pete more choices and compliments, and you are going to visit with the school counselor to discuss some issues going on at home. How about if I give you a call in a week to see how things are progressing. Does that work for you?"

Questions for Reflection

1. Why do you think a fair number of teachers change from being very enthusiastic when they first start teaching to becoming jaded, skeptical, and even cynical as their careers progress?

2. Think of a good salesperson who you like, admire, and buy from regularly. Most good salespeople know their product well, make you feel comfortable, and are able to help you see how your life will be improved in some way that you value if you buy their product or service. When you want something from an administrator, colleague, parent, or student, the same principles apply. You are far more likely to get what you seek when you can successfully consider the following: Put yourself in the other person's shoes and ask yourself how their life is likely to be improved if they do what you ask. Consider the possible obstacles they might face in doing what you ask. Think about how they might address these obstacles successfully.

3. Are you feeling disrespected by a colleague or administrator? What specifically do they say or do? What have you already done? What else might you do with the additional information you have learned?

4. How might you protect yourself from catching a negative attitude from colleagues who never seem to have a nice word to say about anybody? Identify and implement at least two strategies from this section that might turn one of these people around.

5. School climate is largely related to the kind of energy administrators and teachers bring every day. Which colleagues bring positive energy and how do they convey it? If you were in charge of enhancing your school's climate, but only you could act, what would you do differently? Even though your actions might not change the entire school climate, your contribution matters at least a little, and possibly a lot more than you think.

6. Remember a former teacher whose words or deeds made you feel special. Write down what this person said or did. Think about a problem you are currently facing. What advice do you think this teacher might give you? When you are faced with difficult, challenging moments, what kind of support do you appreciate getting from others?

🔑 Key Chapter Thoughts

- Receiving and giving positive feedback is the most powerful tool in creating a school climate conducive to high achievement and happiness.
- To get more of what you want, figure out what other people value or need, and then show them how *their* lives will improve or benefit by doing it your way.
- When you hear or see something that makes you cringe, change the channel before you react.
- Realize you have more control over how you view something than you do over what you are viewing. How we view an issue or person influences how we react to it.
- If you find that your effort to improve things with certain people keeps failing, it is probably best to keep as far away from them as you can.
- At worst, tough parents are misguided or misinformed advocates who really care about their kids. Try to see them in this way.

➡️ For the Administrator

When you have great teachers on staff, the best thing you can do to keep them happy is to give them as much autonomy as possible, get out of their way, and be there when they need you. In his book *Drive*, Daniel Pink (2009) identifies four areas over which leaders can offer employees decision-making authority: task, time, technique, and team. Many excellent teachers feel extremely stifled when they are told not only what students must learn, but also how they must teach. The greatest form of appreciation is a show of respect for their professionalism. Show your great teachers respect by sharing the standards their students must achieve and then allowing teachers to choose the methods they prefer to use to accomplish the end result. Remember, it is rarely the method that matters but rather the teacher who is using the method. You have probably noticed that great teachers get relatively good test scores from their kids no matter what method they use.

When there is team teaching, autonomy over partnering should be encouraged as well. Let teachers choose who to work with unless there is some compelling reason for them to work with someone you select. Because your desire is to retain and reward your best teachers, when circumstances change in their lives, try to accommodate them. For example, if teachers with changed family commitments want to job share, let them. Although scheduling and consistency of instruction can be challenging, really good teachers can usually figure this out. Two great teachers working part-time are a lot better than one mediocre teacher working full-time.

Teachers appreciate having their ideas heard, acknowledged, and whenever possible, implemented. For example, if bullying is an issue at your school, as it is at most, explore with your teachers what they think are the best ways to address this topic. Make yourself available for a before or after school suggestion time. Staff who have thought things out and are serious about their ideas will come while those who like to use up faculty meeting time or suggestion box space to complain won't.

In his book *Good to Great* (2001), Collins cites *humility* and *modesty* alongside *resolve* as key characteristics that distinguish great leaders who achieve results. Great leaders virtually always give credit to others for achieving good results while taking the blame when bad things happen. Don't excuse poor performance but point your finger as much at yourself as at anybody else when things don't go well. Most importantly, buffer teachers whenever you can from having to do the things that draw their attention away from what they love to do. Lots of teachers get sick of the endless paperwork and documentation that seem to benefit nobody but bureaucrats in faraway places. I know budgets are very tight even in good economic times, but try to delegate these responsibilities to office personnel, aides, or volunteers wherever possible.

Let your teachers know that they should expect to be treated respectfully by parents and you are available as a resource whenever they are not. There are some excellent resources available that teach staff how to best handle a variety of situations with challenging parents (Mendler, 2006; Whitaker & Fiore, 2001), yet sometimes even the best approach doesn't work. Teachers need to know you are willing to get your hands dirty on the front lines to support their authority and integrity.

There are many special things you can do for your staff to show appreciation. At one of my elementary schools, the principal hired a few masseuses on a staff development day without telling his staff in advance. The morning portion of the day was devoted to discussion about how to best implement a new schedule, an important but draining process. As the tired teachers were eating lunch, the masseuses set up benches in the hallway. Needless to say, many teachers were thrilled when they left the cafeteria and were greeted in the hallway for a relaxing massage. I know another principal who starts the school year with a staff barbecue at his home. Another has a bi-weekly "Bagels with Bev." There are many little touches like these that can make large differences. Every day look for opportunities to thank your teachers for the work they do through a simple acknowledgment or an occasional thank-you note. Frequently use phrases like "Good point," "Nice job," "Well done," "I really appreciate that," "That's a great question," and "I'm glad you brought that up." It might help for you to keep a log of little wonderful things you see your teachers do that usually go unnoticed. Make a regular habit of acknowledging and appreciating the teachers verbally or with thank-you notes. Consider starting each faculty meeting by asking staff to share appreciations with each other.

Marzano, Waters, and McNulty (2005) suggest using "hard work and results as the basis for rewards and recognition" and "using performance versus seniority as a primary criterion for rewards and recognition" (p. 46). Look for ways to reward your entire staff in honor of an individual teacher's accomplishments. You can do an occasional breakfast, donuts and coffee, or pizzas. Invite all staff to celebrate specific improvements certain classes have made or to share in a special thank-you to the teachers who chaperoned an event, worked on an after-school committee, or mentored troubled students at school. Perhaps even more important is to shield your faculty from the deleterious effects that one or two nasty colleagues can have on everyone's mood. If you are unfortunate enough to have staff members who persistently leave others feeling put down, minimized, de-energized, disrespected, or humiliated, you must confront them and give them an opportunity to change. If they don't and you cannot terminate their employment or transfer them, your actions in confronting them will at least serve to discount the power of these people in the eyes of others.

Approving professional development opportunities keeps your best staff fresh and is a wonderful way to show appreciation. Even though our initial instincts may tell us that this is not cost-effective because good teachers don't really need the additional training, the experience at a good seminar almost always provides at least a jolt of renewal, which can be invaluable. Even the best teachers need occasional validation. Instead of saying to yourself, "She doesn't really need it" consider thinking, "She deserves it." Most research on effective professional development that truly leads to sustained change points to the need for an emphasis on depth and practice (Reeves, 2010). Realistically, a one-day workshop is unlikely to provide depth or practice, but it can be an effective way to provide reinforcement and excitement, which can boost the enthusiasm of your great teachers who are burning out.

When there is conflict among your staff, you may have to be the mediator. Always keep the emphasis on making the school a better place for kids. Staff should know that different views are welcome, and they should be given opportunities to openly share their ideas in a trusting atmosphere. Conflict between staff, as well as between teachers and students, is usually due to some combination of inflexibility, low frustration tolerance, and poor problem-solving skills. Miner, Glomb, and Hulin (2005) found that negative interactions have *five times* the impact on our moods as positive interactions. Think about it: At best, five positive comments are needed to balance one nasty one. Share this with your staff. Positive student confrontation (Curwin, Mendler, & Mendler, 2009) is an effective problem-solving process you can use with staff and between staff and students when conflict occurs. If one of your teachers did something that made you angry, wait to discuss it until you can meet him privately.

In summary, employees who don't receive recognition for their work often become unhappy. Understand how powerful affirmation, recognition, and a little positive feedback from you can be.

CHAPTER FOUR

....

Making the Best of an Imperfect Environment

*Today give all that you have, for what
you keep inside you lose forever.*

Owen Marecic, professional football player

It is sad that in a land rich with resources and great wealth, there are some schools that lack adequate textbooks, supplies, and infrastructure. In some instances, buildings have fallen into disrepair. More commonly there are students who need services and there is not enough money, people, or both to provide the resources. Great teachers can get discouraged by the widespread lack of caring that may exist and the lack of adequate resources to do their job effectively. Have you ever gotten so disgusted at the scrambling you've had to do to get the basics you need that you've thought about throwing in the towel? While most data on job satisfaction is associated with people factors such as the degree of support provided, involvement with others, and the encouragement of innovation, satisfaction with physical working conditions has been shown to be a factor as well (Wells, 2000). Common sense would suggest that if you like where you are going, there is a better chance you'll like what you do when you get there.

Take the Habitat for Humanity Approach

I recently volunteered as a worker on a Habitat for Humanity house after being told that no special skills were required. I thought it would be a cool way to contribute and give back to my community, although I couldn't imagine what they would have me doing. The last time I tried to build something was in seventh grade wood shop class when we had to make a birdhouse. I can still remember shaving a board of wood until there was virtually nothing left of it in an attempt to get one of the sides level. I never did get my birdhouse built. I showed up on my appointed Habitat day along with about a half dozen other people, and within fifteen minutes, I was pounding nails into vinyl siding along with two other white-collar types. We did that all day long. By the way, we were told that if we couldn't or didn't want to do that job, we would be assigned another. I have no idea what the other volunteers did that day, but I do know that every one of them stayed all day and was busy working. I went home about as exhausted as I have ever been, yet I felt fulfilled at having made a small yet meaningful contribution to somebody's life.

Habitat for Humanity is a great example of creating a high quality product at a fraction of the usual cost by using good quality materials and committed volunteers with a wide range of skills and differing levels of commitment who want to make a difference. As far as I know, nobody who wants to help is turned away. Some volunteers come only for a day, others for longer, and a few regularly. Volunteers are supervised by a paid, highly skilled foreman who matches people to jobs and organizes the overall project.

If you work in a school with limited resources, try to think like the highly skilled foreman who has a small budget and a large project. There is a lot that needs to get done, and you need to figure out how to delegate the limited available resources to achieve the best possible result. For the excellent teacher, there is always too much to do and not enough time to do it. You want to reach all of your students all of the time, and needless to say, even when your school is blessed with lots of resources, it is tough to provide for everyone. Some kids carry in lots of baggage from home or the community, so you need to be part social worker. A fair number of students get little support, guidance, or nurturance at home, so you need to be part parent. Some kids are accustomed to getting everything they want without having to do anything to earn it, so they seem bewildered when they are expected to put forth effort. For them, we need to be part boss, disciplinarian, and motivator. Too many kids have no idea how to solve problems with each other, so we also need to be part cop and part mediator. As if all this wasn't enough, virtually all classrooms have students with a huge range of abilities, which requires us to be expert instructional "differentiators." Unless you are lucky and blessed enough to have unlimited resources, there simply aren't enough counselors, psychologists, social workers, and paraprofessionals, nice rooms, adequate supplies, and great instructional coaching. It is not unusual for many teachers to feel the increased burden of buying basic school supplies with money out of their own pocket. With all the effort and personal resources you put forth, it can feel discouraging to lack the support you need to do your job most effectively. It is therefore so important that you stay focused on what is most critical to the students' success (and yours): the knowledge, passion, and caring you bring every day while you scrounge together the stuff you need to give our students the best possible chance.

Identify Resources, Obtain Them, and Delegate

Make a wish list

Like the Habitat foreman, it is important to identify, delegate, and use available people and resources in order to ensure your own well-being and that of your students. Take a moment right now and make a wish list of things and personnel you would like to have (if money were no object) that would give you more of what you need to do your job effectively (e.g., someone to do more one-on-one tutoring; someone to take a walk with an agitated student; a time-out room for disruptive kids; extra pencils, pens, paper, and other supplies). Next, consider people at school (i.e., other students in the classroom, fellow teachers, students from other classes), connected to school (i.e., parents and other family), and organizations (i.e., faith-based groups, businesses, senior citizens, university students) that might be available without cost. Finally, how might you get materials you need donated or at a greatly reduced price? Do you have any responsibilities that you can delegate? What are they? Suggestions, tips, and strategies are offered throughout this section to help you answer these questions so that you can get and effectively use the additional resources you need.

You are the most important resource

Just yesterday, my daughter, who is doing an internship in social work, was complaining that her agency offered little privacy to conduct interviews. When a private room could be found, it was often a large, cold conference room. I reminded her that while this was not the ideal situation, *she* was the most important object in the room that would determine whether her clients feel sufficiently comfortable to share personal details of their lives.

As noted earlier, the renowned educational researcher John Goodlad looked at 40 years of educational innovations while at UCLA and did not find a single one that increased student achievement. The only factor that increased achievement was the effectiveness of the teacher. After donating millions of dollars to establish small learning academies that were touted by researchers as the way to better achievement, The Bill and Melinda Gates Foundation switched gears and instead provides support to identify effective instructional practices. I don't dismiss the potential benefits of a small school or small class size in building relationships or differentiating instruction. It is nice to walk inside a modern school with all the amenities, but at the end of the day, it is you the teacher and what you do that matters most. As the excellent teacher you are or want to become, remember that during this difficult time!

Some people defy the odds and do great things despite getting little support of any kind. Efren Peñaflorida Jr., winner of the 2009 CNN Heroes Award, is a great example. He began on his own in 1997 in a shantytown of Cavite, Philippines, with a plastic bag containing some books and school supplies. He taught children who had little if any formal education in impoverished gang-infested neighborhoods. This has evolved into a "pushcart classroom" that is a mini-classroom with a mini-library, reading aids, blackboards, and even detachable tables and chairs. Today, ten thousand youth volunteers go around with these carts teaching reading, writing, and arithmetic as well as values like discipline, persistence, and good hygiene. Clearly, Peñaflorida and his army of volunteers work in anything but ideal conditions. Although it is great to have top-notch tools, remember that you are the most important tool your students have.

Use your colleagues

I was cruising around an inner-city elementary school in one of the toughest areas of Milwaukee, trying to help teachers learn and adopt more effective disciplinary practices. The principal suggested that along the way I drop in on Mr. Sanders's sixth grade class. When I did, I was astounded to observe approximately 60 well-behaved students completely engaged in a lesson with Mr. Sanders, who was the only adult present. A substitute teacher could not be found to cover a fifth-grade teacher's absence that day, so Mr. Sanders agreed to teach that class in addition to his own. I stayed for about 20 minutes and watched in amazement as this maestro elicited a symphony of learning from his students without a hiccup. The kids were motivated, polite, on-task, and well behaved, in stark contrast to what was going on in several other classrooms. I couldn't help but wonder why this school had hired me as an outside consultant when they had in their midst one of the most incredible and willing teachers that I have ever seen. When I asked him later on if he had ever shared his ideas and strategies with other staff, he told me that he felt dismissed by most of his colleagues, who didn't want to listen to him.

Other professionals like doctors and lawyers regularly create partnerships so that they can consult with each other on difficult cases. Is it a false sense of pride, embarrassment to ask for help, or a desire to not bother others that makes many teachers underutilize colleagues for support? Although the reasons may vary, there are all kinds of ways other teachers can help you make your life easier, and you can help them as well. When I was teaching there were times that I needed to get some space from certain students, but that wasn't an option. Most teachers know that usually their most difficult students have the best attendance. They are always there! Anyway, sometimes their behavior makes it impossible to teach, but more often you just need a break from them. With three colleagues, I worked out an arrangement where we could send students to each other for a break if we needed one. If a student arrived with a white envelope from one of us, it meant simply to thank the student and send him right back. Whoever did the sending just needed a momentary break. A sealed blue envelope meant strangulation fantasies were setting in (just kidding, although you know what I mean). The receiving colleague was to open the envelope and then have that student remain with her for the next several minutes to offer a longer break. Usually kids will behave for somebody else in an unfamiliar environment for a short period of time. Although we didn't use each other very often, knowing we could was a godsend. Similarly, even the best teachers occasionally have trouble with certain students or certain classes. Check with your colleagues to see if anybody is having more success than you are, and if somebody is, ask her what she is doing. I remember doing that, and my colleague told me that the kid who was a problem for me generally did a lot better when he had a daily agenda that specified tasks/assignments/activities and time allotted for each. I did that and saw improvement almost immediately. Counselors, psychologists, and social workers can be immensely helpful in getting a handle on what makes certain kids or groups tick. Check with them when you are stumped. Many times, fine-tuning something simple can make all the difference.

Form or use a PLC

Professional learning communities (PLC) have become increasingly popular as a way for schools to encourage continuous learning and collaboration among staff. If your school is a professional learning community, there are processes that already exist to encourage the regular sharing of ideas and best practices. If not, form your own informal professional learning community (DuFour, DuFour, Eaker, & Many, 2006). One way is to start a book study group around a certain topic that is likely to be of interest to other teachers at your school. There a number of ways the group can be organized. The most popular ways are either for all to read a chapter of the book each week and have a group discussion, or for a few individuals to be assigned a chapter, highlight the key points or strategies, and share them at a weekly meeting. The larger goal of a PLC is to facilitate high levels of learning for all students by having teachers work collaboratively and engage in "collective inquiry" with colleagues. Teachers share best practices with each other from their own experience and from knowledge gleaned from within and outside the school. Regular meetings are part of the process because strategies and interventions need continuous monitoring to ensure success.

One caveat about professional learning communities: I have visited a few PLC schools that were taught to grade only work, never behavior. Although this is a sensible recommendation for many, there may be times when grading behavior makes sense. For example, if a class has students with poor interpersonal skills who call out whenever they want or whose every other comment in class to each other is "shut up," grading behavior might make a lot of sense. Otherwise, nobody is likely to get much work done. Apparently some PLC trainers are dogmatic about what practices can and cannot be done in school, based upon the "research." As any good educator knows, there is no educational research about anything that can make a 100 percent claim. A "good" decision is made by a team of educators (in most cases with student participation as well) after reviewing the likely pros and cons, is educationally sound, and is relevant to the issue at that school.

Use other students in your class

One great way to teach students responsibility is to give them choices and a feeling of ownership. You also benefit because the more students do for themselves in the classroom, the less you have to do for them. Organizational tasks that you might consider tedious, boring, and time-consuming can often be delegated to your students. Assign or have students choose jobs that need to get done in order for the classroom to run as efficiently as possible. Identify jobs that you know need to be done, and then invite your students to brainstorm others they think are needed. These might include class greeter, errand runner, paper distributor, assignment collector, regional quieter, materials supplier, office informer, work hanger, dispute mediator, cheerer upper, line leader, pet feeder, rules reminder, and playground captain. Add to the list. How do you feel knowing that all of these tasks and others can likely be handled by students and probably enjoyed by them with minimal oversight by you?

Use students from other classes

From about second grade and up, individual attention and assistance can be provided by older students. It is usually best to team
with teachers at least two grade levels above you. You pair students
who need help in academics (e.g., reading), personal care (e.g.,
help getting boots on at the end of the day), or social skills (e.g.,
making friends) with older students who are already skilled in
these areas or those who could benefit from the experience of being
a helper. Challenging students are usually a very good choice to
be helpers because these kids tend to get a lot out of these experiences by learning they can make a difference in a positive way. They
enthusiastically embrace the responsibility because it represents a
sharp contrast with their usual school lives most often character-
ized by either being in trouble or getting rather than giving help.
Older students helping younger ones is therefore a winning combination for both students and teachers. You benefit from getting an
extra pair of hands, and your colleague benefits from the temporary
absence of their troubling students. Be sure to oversee specific tasks.
Because there is at least a two-grade-level separation, the older kids
can be put to help in a variety of ways.

Use retired teachers, police, fire, and military personnel

Teachers, police officers, firefighters, and military personnel are
often relatively young when they retire and are therefore often
vigorous, eager, and community-oriented. They have been around
challenging situations and often make for excellent companions
for kids. Students who need guidance can benefit from being
paired with such a volunteer. Go to the firehouse, police station,
and military recruiting post to let folks there know that you would
love to have their retired professionals involved in your class. You
might also consider approaching the Elks, Lions, and Masons to

explore involving their members in doing some of the tasks you wish you had more time to do with some of your students. It is best to be prepared with specific roles you are looking for volunteers to fulfill in order for things to work best.

Know and use your community resources

Tucked away in the basement of a mid-city urban high school that I recently visited was a small community resources office that had many informational brochures from agencies and organizations ranging from Alcoholics Anonymous to police athletic leagues. There was a counselor present but very little student activity. I was surprised because it seemed to me that there were probably many students at the school who could benefit from these resources. Later on, when I asked teachers if they referred students to this office or tried to partner with any of the community organizations that were represented, I was astounded to learn that few even knew such an office existed at their school.

It requires little insight to realize that schools cannot alone address the many complex and diverse needs of students. In virtually every community, there are a substantial number of people eager to volunteer their time for worthy causes and free local resources available to support what you are trying to do in your classroom. Most communities have Boys/Girls clubs, Big Brothers/Big Sisters, police athletic leagues, and faith-based organizations eager to lend a hand. It is in your interest and that of your students to learn who these organizations are, what they do, and how they may be able to help.

Many businesses are often eager to provide financial support, free labor, or mentors. An article appearing in *USA Today* indicated that in recessionary times, companies are more likely to give products and time off for employees to volunteer in lieu of money. For example, Bank of America pledged to donate one million volunteer hours by the end of 2010. Their goal was to top the 800,000 hours they donated the prior year. In collaboration with Heart of America,

Target renovated 19 school libraries in 2009 and 32 more in 2010. More than 150,000 IBM employees contributed more than ten million hours of service in the past five years. According to Alison Rose of the Committee Encouraging Corporate Philanthropy, "more than 90 percent of companies offer some type of formal volunteer employee program" (Garton, 2010). Try to get a local business to adopt your class. Realize that this is a good business practice for them as well as a source of support for you and your kids. I am partial to businesses that have pictures of the Little League baseball team they sponsor. Although I am sure many sponsors do this out of the goodness of their hearts, probably at least as many do it because it is good for their business. Imagine how good it would look for a picture of your class to be prominently displayed in Skip's Meat Market with the kids wearing t-shirts bearing their name.

> *Suggestion:* Make a list of all the supplies and support you wish you had that would enable you to do your job more effectively. Now consider the specific ways that you would use these supplies or people in the classroom. What activities would you want them to assist you with? Are there certain students you would target? How would you plan to use the supplies to accomplish instructional goals? After completing your list and answering these questions, try to identify and then contact a few of the businesses, agencies, and organizations that provide these resources. I know many teachers are uncomfortable when they feel like salesmen. But realize that most community groups and businesses want to be identified with education in a positive way.

Getting needed supplies

For "little" things like book bags, backpacks, pencils, notebook paper, blank CDs or DVDs, stickers and other goodies, office supply stores are often willing to donate or at least sell at a reduced cost. Get to know the manager at your local Staples, Office Max, and Wal-Mart. Tell them about your kids and explore not only the supplies that they might give, but also what they can get. Perhaps you can trigger an interest in having them "adopt your class." There is so much enrichment for people to gain from tutoring and mentoring. You might also try to initiate a partnership with a wealthier school through a friend who might be teaching there. Have your kids get to know theirs. Over time, relationships will develop and help can be sought. There are many good-hearted people willing to provide resources if asked.

Consider periodically taking up collections from kids in your class when you are low on school supplies. If your students have extras at home, you can suggest they donate a few pencils, pens, papers, or notebooks for classmates who might have forgotten theirs. Keep these supplies for kids who come unprepared or who may not be able to afford their own. Seek donations periodically from your students if and when supplies get low. Encourage all students to bring something to class that could be of assistance to others, especially if they borrowed supplies brought by somebody else. At open house, let parents know the supplies needed for their kids to be successful. At the same time, remind them that extras (be specific) are appreciated since some families might be less able to provide. You might initiate a schoolwide program in which parents and others within the community can donate money or necessary items in short supply. Your school's PTA can be a valuable resource for this pursuit. Consider doing 50/50 fund-raising auctions once or twice a year among your school community and friends. People donate money with tickets sold for a fixed amount, and then there is a drawing with the winner claiming half the money and you getting the other half. Be sure to first check with administration to ensure that proper district and legal guidelines are followed.

Seek corporate sponsors

Although controversial, I think the practice of selling direct advertising such as Channel One is very underutilized by schools. Especially in an era of budget tightening, it is inexcusable to not use every resource possible to obtain the funds needed for all kinds of things that states and municipalities are unable to fund. Corporate sponsorship is a diamond awaiting exploitation. Like a sports arena that sells every bit of space for advertising, consider how much money could be raised by selling advertising space or naming rights. Classrooms, hallways, the cafeteria, the gym, faculty lounge, administrative offices all could be named. Many of these same locations could provide advertising space. How about advertising on school buses? Cities raise money by selling advertising on municipal buses and subways. Why not schools? Think about how many more supplies might be donated if the donor's name was on the notebook, pencil, or computer. Just as a corporation sponsors a little league team, they could sponsor a classroom and have their name on the door with the teacher's name underneath. Naturally, you will need the approval of higher-ups to pursue such initiatives. Ideally, this is something that would occur at a school or district level.

The argument that children are vulnerable or defenseless against advertisements intended to influence their behavior has some merit. But, on balance, the opportunities to obtain funds from numerous sources to compensate for tight school budgets vastly outweighs the possible deleterious effect advertising may have on youth. Let's face it—kids are exposed to so many ads from so many sources from a very early age. Seeing a few more at school is unlikely to play much of an influence on shaping them. But to ensure good taste, a committee could be set up to vet the ads and businesses. To those who might argue that this is more trouble than it is worth, that it would add more to the plate of already busy educators or that a whole new bureaucracy would be needed to evaluate the moral worthiness of advertisers, I would counter that if enough money could be raised, wouldn't it be worth the investment? To others concerned that such a practice would move schools away from "democratic" values to "market" values, I feel confident that both can coexist just as they do coexist in life outside of school.

Compensate with Technology

Use technology and attend webinars

If you work at a school with a limited budget and resources, expand your knowledge by attending relatively inexpensive webinars. These are online video or audio presentations of relatively short duration on a wide range of topics relevant to educators that are often given by leading experts in the field. All you need is access to a computer. For a nominal fee, you can watch or listen to the presentation in real time and/or have access for a period thereafter (usually between one and two weeks). There is a lot of specific information offered in a one hour time frame that allows you comfort and flexibility. I have given webinars on several topics that have included an opportunity for participants to ask questions live or through e-mail for up to two weeks after. Check out these websites for more information on attending webinars for teachers: ascd.org and tlc-sems.com.

Yet another "high-tech" option to keep current and get information that may be relevant and useful is to use Facebook or Twitter. You can network with numerous educators who are blogging about virtually every subject imaginable. Once you familiarize yourself with Twitter and develop a relevant network, you can obtain good information without spending hours surfing. Anyone can set up a free account by visiting http://twitter.com.

To increase contact with parents so they have rapid access to important information about their children, your school can acquire parentCONNECT. This is an online tool that enables parents to easily communicate with teachers via e-mail or receive automatic e-mail announcements of unexcused absences, missing assignments, discipline referrals, and failing grades. Parents can also obtain school announcements as well as their student's schedules, grades, assignments, course history, and health/immunization data.

Use cell phones as instructional devices

As a general strategy, consider legitimizing behaviors that occur at a very high rate but with limits. We have all heard the phrase, "If you can't beat them, join them." This is a good practice to consider when a problem is occurring at such a high rate that it is either impossible or impractical to change. Most schools ban cell phones but many students bring and use them anyway. Many students are so adept at texting that they can appear to be paying attention to a lesson while having an extensive texting conversation. Consider legitimizing cell phones! Instead of banning them, require students to keep them visible during class. If you can see cell phones, that gives you a much better way of monitoring their use.

Even better, use them instructionally. A high school teacher I know in Nebraska requires her students to bring cell phones to class and use them to store class and homework assignments. Ferriter (2010) offers a number of instructional suggestions including collecting data with multiple choice and open-ended surveys. Students can use their cell phones to access information they need when working on projects. Cell phones can serve as calculators, dictionaries, and encyclopedias. Look at their presence as a resource that virtually all kids have that can replace or serve as an alternative for resources that can be difficult to obtain during tight budget times. It is a tool that huge numbers of people, particularly minorities, already use to access the Internet for information. According to a Pew Research Poll (Smith, 2010), 51 percent of Hispanics and 46 percent of African Americans use their phones as their primary device to access the Internet compared to 33 percent of whites. Using technology that students and teachers are already familiar with for academic purposes might be a great equalizer in providing access to information that is so crucial for achieving high academic performance, particularly with students who might otherwise lack access to top notch educational resources.

In addition to our students using their cell phones to chat with each other or listen to music, let's focus their use at school on discussing ideas, obtaining information, talking to people who they otherwise would not be able to talk to, and conducting research on a wide variety of topics. For example, the Google Wonder Wheel helps people focus their searches by breaking down large ideas and concepts into manageable groups of related websites. This feature can quickly point your students in new directions and provides a very helpful way to organize material around virtually any issue. The Wonder Wheel feature can be found on the left side of any Google search. However, before allowing cell phone access in your classroom, you may need to seek a change of school rules or at least a waiver that allows you to implement a practice usually banned by a rule.

Use interactive technology

Teachers have been using collaboration through active or cooperative learning for a long time. Arguably, with this approach the chief benefit for students is the social factor that gets paired with learning. An interactive whiteboard can take interactive learning to an entirely different level. Whiteboards are underutilized in schools probably due to their complexity and the lack of inservice training by manufacturers. Fortunately, within the last few years, these devices have become more user-friendly and less expensive, and can often be easily integrated into the curriculum to create lessons that improve class participation and student attention. Although I am not recommending a particular system (because technology advances so rapidly) I have observed kids with enthusiastic teachers in cramped and otherwise uninviting classroom conditions achieve impressive results and maintain high energy while using the Mobi whiteboard and CPS Pulse student response system.

Maximizing Other Resources

Record your classes

To maximize how effective things can be in your class, consider video recording specific lessons or segments and then review the recording. Are you using the limited space you have in the best possible way to accomplish your goals? Which students are leaning forward, looking engaged? Who is slouched back? Are the students participating in their own learning or are you doing it all? Do you do all the talking? When do the kids seem most or least on task? There is a lot you can learn about yourself and your students in this way. If there is an instructional coach at your school, ask the coach to watch with you and offer constructive criticism. You could ask a colleague as well. It might well be eye-opening for you to share the recording with your students for specific reasons. For example, you might ask them to look for or count the number of times students asked a question, participated in discussion, blurted something out, or got out of their seats. You might ask them to tell you what you did that helped them learn or made it harder for them to learn.

Be a student for a day

Sometimes it can be helpful to step outside one's familiar role to see things from a new perspective. The popular television show *Undercover Boss* takes the viewer through a week in the life of a CEO who acts as a new hire in a variety of jobs at the company. The CEO experiences the complexity of other jobs at the company, and he gets to see good and bad practices among his employees. At Beth Israel Hospital in Boston, doctors sometimes dress as maintenance staff and cruise through the floors. This accomplishes two purposes: it gives them a taste of what it is like to be a support staff employee and helps them find ways to improve the hospital environment.

I am familiar with a school in Kentucky that requires its teachers to be students for a day. There is a twofold purpose very much like the hospital: to sensitize teachers to the student experience and to identify ways to improve the school environment based upon insights teachers gain from being students. Although it is impossible to completely enter the role of student due to age differences, teachers ride the bus to school, dress like students, travel to class as students, and eat lunch in the student cafeteria. When they are in class as a student, they have to follow the same rules as the students. To minimize distractions to learning that would be caused by several teachers pretending to be students on a specific day, only one or two teachers has the experience on any given day. Teachers at this school find that they often gain a tremendous amount of knowledge leading to the identification of strategies that can improve school climate.

Consider initiating this practice, particularly if you are wondering if there are certain policies or practices that could make your school a better place. Other than the expense for one or two substitutes, this is a very inexpensive way to identify areas needing school improvement. Once problems are identified, staff (and perhaps students as well) can work together to explore solutions.

Expand your use of grades to include behavior

There are certain student behaviors that can worsen an already challenging atmosphere. For example, there are too many daily interruptions in most schools over which teachers have little to no control: fire drills, paging students on the intercom, students who need extra help leaving to go elsewhere in the middle of a lesson while others are returning. These interruptions often need to be addressed at a schoolwide level, and you should think about ways of bringing this to the attention of administrators or whatever decision-making committee might exist at school. But the most frequent interruptions faced by most teachers are students either breaking rules or not following procedures. Consider giving daily grades to help you shape the behavior you need to see. Ideally, this grade would be separate from a grade earned for academic performance. However, if there is no such option, make behavior a minor but meaningful part of the grade. Be careful to identify only behaviors that are crucial to the teaching and learning process for consideration. For example, if lateness is a problem, which obviously impacts instructional time, you might give students a *T* for being on time. After students receive 10 *T*s, they get a 100% quiz grade that gets averaged into all their other grades (the system you devise should have behavior count for no more than 10–15 percent of a student's overall grade). I have found that it usually works best to provide a grading incentive for the desired behavior rather than diminishing a grade because of inappropriate behavior. Although this won't completely solve the problem, it will slow the leak.

A classwide application of this strategy is good if there are several students who are breaking a rule. For example, let's say you have five students who are often late. Set up a procedure so that if fewer than five are late, the entire class except those who were late gets an *A*. When students receive 10 *A*s they get a 100% quiz grade. Modify the time frame and the criteria to realistically fit your students. If necessary you can further individualize when you are doing this with your entire class. For example, you might establish a "10-day" criterion with your class, but with your chronic kids who are never there on time, 10 may feel unachievable. Approach them individually, and lower the number for them (e.g., three on-times each week with an extra *A* for a perfect week). If other students complain, remind them that you will talk to them only about them, not about others. Reinforce the difference between being fair and treating everybody exactly the same way.

Set up structured, enjoyable activities

Although not a direct result of inadequate resources, teaching kids after lunch is often the most difficult time of the day because of the chaos lunch often causes. Consider either changing the schedule or the activities during lunch in order to impact this problem.

The most orderly cafeteria I ever visited was at Victor Intermediate School in Rochester, New York. The secret to their success was understanding that third through fifth grade students do not need forty minutes to eat their lunch. Ten minutes is usually sufficient. Through the leadership of their principal, they planned activities to follow lunch. Some were staffed by teachers but many were run by parent volunteers. The school recruited parents and staff who had interests or hobbies to share with students. Some of the interests or hobbies were for one session but most were ongoing (e.g., once a week). A few were daily (e.g., playing checkers and chess; quiet study time). Students signed up for each week's activities in their class and then after they finished their lunch they would head off to their chosen destination. A portion of the cafeteria was used, as were rooms and spaces that were adjacent to the cafeteria so as to avoid the confusion that could be caused by excess movement.

There is clearly a considerable amount of planning required to establish a program of this magnitude. But if chaos is the norm during the less structured parts of the school day, it may well be worth the effort.

> *Suggestion:* In your own classroom, consider doing a modified version of the schoolwide approach used at Victor Intermediate School. Give your students a homework assignment that requires them to interview their parents, family members or neighbors to learn about hobbies or interests they have that they might be willing to share with the class. Have your students write or report about the interest, event, experience, or hobby and ask them to include contact information of the person who shared it. Ask the adults if they might be willing to visit your class to

share their experience or talent. You can ask them to send you an e-mail listing available times. Then plan a schedule that brings these folks into your classroom. It will often enliven things or at least briefly change the tone.

Make your class what you want it to be

Think of a store or a place that you love to be. Really try to visualize the sights, sounds and smells. Are other people around? What are you or they doing? What are the characteristics of the people or place that makes you want to be there? Be guided by what you find welcoming. For example, what makes you shop in certain stores? How do the employees treat you while you are in the store? Are they friendly or do they ignore you? Does it depend, and what does it depend upon? What is the lighting like? Is there music in the background? Are the walls plain or decorated? What is the quality of the merchandise? Are you allowed to handle things or are you even encouraged to handle things? Are you free to explore or must you ask permission? Do you have to wait very long for assistance or is the service accommodating? If you make a mistake, how do people react?

Write down your answers. Most people who do this exercise give answers like the following: they have what I want, people treat me with respect, the place is really nice (e.g., brightly colored, pleasant sounds or sights, you can easily find what you want, it is fun). The most popular answer is "It is a warm, welcoming place where I feel cared about."

How do the characteristics above relate to your classroom? Which aspects do you believe you can arrange that are conducive to the learning that needs to go on in the classroom? Most people learn best when they like being where they are. Set up your classroom to add as many of these features as you possibly can. If you make your place into a place where you want to be and your students want to be, good things usually happen. If you are concerned that other staff might disapprove of your vision, be brave enough to not care. After all, if doing it their way was working well for you, you probably would not be reading this book!

Brighten things up

Do whatever you can to brighten the mood in your classroom. If the lighting is dull, see if the custodian can help you install brighter lights. Maybe the walls could use a cheerier paint and some cool artwork. Maybe there are some graffiti artists among your students who can suggest some tasteful ways to decorate. Perhaps you can hook up with the art department to get some suggestions and some artists to redesign the room. You might explore how you can involve your class in designing and painting a mural based on subject area content or academic theme. Some schools have beautiful murals decorating the halls or individual classrooms. Think about using some mood music in your classroom. Classical music at low volume is a good choice when students are working either individually or in small groups. Rap and hip-hop is a better choice when you want to generate some extra energy. Consider creating a quiet corner of the classroom that can be furnished with bean bag chairs or something similar.

I know that I have no eye for interior design, so when I want to improve the look of my home I check in with a few people whose homes I love. I figure that they can help me figure out what can be done with the space I have that fits my taste. Check out other classrooms to get some ideas about how you might beautify yours. Ask teachers who seem to have decorative tastes that appeal to you for help or invite a neighbor or friend with design skills to your classroom to give you some ideas. Some people love designing or redesigning space and might be happy to lead the effort as a volunteer. Additionally, give strong consideration to involving your students in "beautification" projects. It is a way to give them some responsibility and a source of free labor.

Change things around occasionally

Every so often, give your classroom a new look. Hang up different pictures. Rearrange the furniture or the seating configuration. Involve your students in the process. Let their creativity take hold. It can be fun for them to think of ways they can enliven the environment around them. One or two students might want to bring in their small pet. Consider how you might use plants, flowers, and even aromas to make things look and feel better. If your classroom lacks adequate lighting, painting the classroom with a lighter, brighter color can help. There might be ways to enhance the lighting with brighter halogen bulbs. Ask if your classroom can accommodate additional lighting. You would likely be easily able to get donated lamps from a variety of sources.

Questions for Reflection

1. An example in this section refers to a teacher in an inner-city school in Milwaukee who was effectively teaching 60 inner-city 5th graders alone. He had limited supplies and far from the latest technological support. You are already a great teacher or aspiring to become one. Because there are probably no more resources or supplies available on days when things are going well, what is it that makes the difference on the good days?

2. What ways can you think of to use students as resources? Since most students like to feel "in charge," what things have to get done each day that can be delegated to them?

3. What ways can you use other colleagues as resources? Is there a colleague you admire who seems able to make do with limited resources? Can you find out more about how he or she does it?

4. Most parents are eager to do whatever is necessary to help their children succeed. How might you connect more effectively with your PTO to gain more supplies or assistance? Where else

might you go within the community to seek additional supplies or resources?

5. Sometimes we have technological resources that could be used to assist with instruction but we just don't think about them or know how to use them. Using cell phones within instruction is an example. Other times, when our creativity flourishes, solutions can be found that would have seemed unlikely. Were there any technological or creative ideas shared in this chapter that you liked but dismissed as "impractical"? Because it is unlikely that there will be a sudden infusion of money that will give you all the resources you need, challenge yourself to get beyond the "impractical." You might find solutions that will make things better for you and your students.

Key Chapter Thoughts

• Use students in your class, students in other classes, colleagues, volunteers, and community resources to help compensate for inadequate support and resources. Like a Goodwill store that collects necessities from volunteer donors, perhaps you can organize a "donation" night at school where specifically requested items are contributed.

• For little things like book bags, backpacks, pencils, notebook paper, blank CDs or DVDs, stickers, and other goodies, office supply stores are often willing to donate or at least sell at a reduced cost.

• Corporate sponsorship is a diamond awaiting exploitation. Sports arenas sell every bit of space for advertising—consider how much money your school could raise by selling advertising space or naming rights. There are numerous possibilities, including the school office, hallways, cafeteria, auditorium, and trophy case.

• If you work at a school with a limited budget and resources, expand your knowledge by attending relatively inexpensive webinars.

- Consider legitimizing cell phones! Instead of banning them, require students to keep cell phones visible during class. Even better, use them instructionally. For example, have students take pictures of important notes with their cell phones.
- Every so often, give your classroom a new look. Hang up different pictures. Rearrange the furniture or the seating configuration. Involve your students in the process. Let their creativity take hold.

➡ For the Administrator

Some years ago, as I was pondering my future, one of the principals I worked with suggested that I give school administration some thought. He was a well-respected and admired leader in a school with limited resources who had brought about some impressive changes with a veteran and highly outspoken staff. At the same time, he was a highly stressed guy who drank about 15 cups of coffee a day and attended endless meetings primarily with people disgruntled about one thing or another, or to hear about the latest standards, policies, or procedures handed down by bureaucrats hundreds of miles away that had to be implemented and over which he had no control. His day started before dawn and rarely ended before eight at night. I wondered if he ever got to see the sun shine.

Since then, I have come to realize that to run a successful school takes a yeoman's effort even with the best of resources, and far from all schools have the best of resources. But with fewer resources, more falls on you to create and sustain a positive school climate where students succeed and teachers flourish. A major part of your job is to figure out ways of maximizing the resources you do have and minimizing the distractions to make the lives of your teachers easier. You want their energy focused on teaching rather than on filling out paperwork, looking for supplies, seeking adequate work space, or spending their weekends scavenging at garage sales finding stuff to enhance the look of their classroom. As a result, while this section of the book is the shortest for teachers, it might be the longest for you. Hopefully, these tips will help.

As school budgets tighten and an era of tight fiscal restraint lies ahead, it will become more and more necessary to seek and use community volunteers and corporate sponsorships to sustain and expand school programs. One of the strategies described in the section for teachers identifies a variety of ways to seek financial support from businesses through the sale of advertising and naming rights. I envision the school principal needing to increasingly network and partner with community groups, faith-based organizations, and businesses to provide the labor and money for initiatives that are good for kids and teachers but are not included in the budget. Many organizations are especially willing to help when they see how their involvement is likely to bring positive attention to them. Even more are interested when they think increased sales are likely. While I can appreciate the angst one might feel in opening this door, consider the fact that most reputable nonprofit institutions like universities and hospitals name buildings, labs, and "chairs" for individual or corporate sponsors. In fact, many hire a "development" individual or department whose sole job is to raise money. Why not us? Don't our kids and teachers deserve top-notch facilities and tools? Lead the way!

Far and away the best resource for teachers is other teachers. Yet rarely do teachers get to share practical ideas and strategies with each other. Make this collaboration a priority. Time for planning and strategizing is especially needed when there is a change in school philosophy or procedure. For example, the schools that successfully transitioned to block schedules virtually always provided teachers with curriculum methods and time for planning to ensure that the extended period would be filled meaningfully. To run an effective block, with rare exception, the teacher should plan for no more than 10 to 15 minutes of an activity or type of instruction. So for a 90-minute block, somewhere between four and six activities or types of instruction are needed to keep students involved and motivated. Many teachers need ideas to productively fill that time. The number one use for your faculty meetings should be to address this type of need. Frankly, if there aren't specific strategies or practical methods shared at a faculty meeting, then it is a good bet that the meeting was a waste of time. When educators come to learn about discipline or motivation at my seminars, they virtually always identify the portions of the conference when they shared strategies with each other as the most beneficial. Make this happen at your school. It is very easy for teachers to feel isolated and disconnected from their peers during a typical school day. For teachers to grow, they need to be around each other. Encourage your teachers to form professional support groups to cull ideas from each other or to discuss ways to implement policies. Be open to different topics that they need to learn more about and then work to arrange for them to be together. This may require rearranging the school schedule and hiring substitute teachers to "float." However, many schools have created innovative ways for teachers and administrators to get together regularly. Carver (2004) wrote about Kalamazoo High School's Maroon Club for new teachers. They meet every two weeks with one of the school administrators to focus on learning about teaching and tackling real problems of practice. As a school psychologist at Crane Elementary School in Rochester, New York, I led a monthly after-school support group for educators. We discussed instructional and behavioral issues teachers faced and then collaboratively brainstormed ideas and solutions. The energy in the group was usually electric, transforming some tired, overwhelmed colleagues at the end of a school day into a reinvigorated, hopeful bunch who left with a combination of new ideas and a belief that they were on the right track.

MetLife's 2009 Survey of the American Teacher found that teachers in schools with higher levels of collaborative activities were more likely than others to have high levels of career satisfaction. The same survey found that 17 percent of teachers were likely to leave the teaching profession within five years. This number was down from 26 percent three years earlier. The authors attributed the downward trend not to more satisfied teachers, but rather to changed economic conditions. This suggests that more "dissatisfied" teachers are likely to stay longer, implying that more will need to be done to increase job satisfaction for a greater number of teachers. Because there is a relationship between teacher empowerment and job satisfaction, leadership and collaborative opportunities are likely to move the conversation in the right direction. Encourage and invite creativity from your staff. If a solution is proposed or a method suggested that doesn't at first seem reasonable (e.g., legitimizing cell phones), resist the impulse to dismiss it. Explore it. Get inside it. If you still have your doubts, allow it for a brief trial period. Great teachers need to feel that their "outside the box" ideas have a decent chance of being implemented if they present a compelling case.

Providing stimulating and effective professional development is yet another way to keep yourself and your best teachers motivated. Go out of your way to approve training opportunities for them. Fundraising may become increasingly necessary for this purpose since this is a "line item" more likely to get cut in tight fiscal times. Before they attend, take the time to meet and discuss what you and they hope to learn from the training. After they attend, take time to meet and explore what they learned and how they intend to apply it to their teaching. Have them share what they learned with other staff. Your goal should be to have most PD teacher-led. This can be much more cost-effective and motivational since the teacher-leader feels respected, rewarded, and empowered. They are also much more likely to be able to make the information more "user-friendly" to colleagues by adapting it to fit your school setting.

There are many relevant topics for educators that can be addressed through inexpensive, easily accessible webinars. These are usually offered after school so there is no release time or need for substitutes. All or some of your staff can attend for the same price. Teachers can access the information either in real time or during a limited period after the event. Encourage your teachers to check these out and support their attendance by providing the nominal financial support, if possible. If you haven't done so already, it is advisable for you to familiarize yourself with Twitter by setting up a free account so you can network with other educators who are dealing with issues and sharing solutions that you will undoubtedly find interesting and helpful. Your familiarity will also enable you to recommend specific sites to your staff.

Many schools have adopted the practice of book study as a component of staff development. Either all or some faculty read a book on an issue of importance and then get together to share ideas, strategies, and questions chapter by chapter. If it is an easy read, all can read the entire book by a certain date. If it is more detailed, readings can be broken down chapter by chapter with individuals or small groups assigned a portion. If there is credit assigned, you could have participants prepare book or chapter reports that speak to the essence of what they learned, what they think can be easily implemented, and what needs further study.

Encourage your best teachers to record instruction and to open up their classrooms so others can see them demonstrate elements of an effective lesson, differentiation strategy, or behavioral intervention. You might encourage weaker teachers to visit the classes of excellent teachers for a specific purpose. Let them know that you will check in with them after the observation to ask them for details about what they saw and learned. You can also make your excellent teachers available to visit the classrooms of colleagues who are struggling, to help them implement changed practices. Offer to cover their classes while they are visiting. When teachers see colleagues experiencing greater success in similar working conditions, it is easier for them to realize that it is primarily the teacher's skills rather than the conditions that are most important.

Make it a point to eliminate all unnecessary interruptions (like announcements and removal of students for noninstructional purposes) during instructional time. Except for something major, loudspeakers should remain silent during class. I was recently at a school where the nurse interrupted class to give students hearing tests. Every 10 minutes or so, four kids left and four returned, making for lots of unnecessary chaos. This is something that could have been done during lunch and spaced out over however many days were necessary. Interrupt instruction only for urgent matters.

Faculty meetings can be a source for obtaining useful information or an annoyance. If you are going to call a meeting, be sure that it is productive. Fewer, shorter, well-focused meetings can serve important functions. They can provide a chance for teachers from different departments or grade levels to communicate, cooperate, and solve problems. They provide a forum for staff with different perspectives to learn from each other and to see the bigger picture, such as schoolwide objectives rather than individual or grade-level goals. At the beginning of the meeting, state the goal or goals and then don't deviate. Put a strict time limit on the duration of the meeting to keep things moving. Keep them short—in the neighborhood of a half-hour or less. Stay focused on the agenda, inviting those who want to bring up something unrelated or who simply like to gripe to see you before or after school. Start the meeting on time. To encourage everyone to be there on time, consider some kind of incentive, like those who are on time participate in a raffle drawing that entitles the winner to a period in which you teach their class while they relax. Or you could implement a penalty for late comers, such as a few dollars that could be collected and donated to charity (or for donuts). Set limits regarding the use of cell phones. Don't allow people to interrupt each other. If somebody gripes or tries to change the subject, invite them to see you during your "before school" time. As mentioned earlier, let your faculty know the day or days you get in early and tell them they are welcome to make suggestions or share concerns at that time. That practice eliminates all but those who feel deeply about an issue, since people who like to complain or just hear themselves talk will rarely make the sacrifice to come early. If the purpose of the meeting was to change something, before the meeting ends, it is crucial to identify three Ws: What needs to be done next, Who is going to do it, and When will it get done. Be sure to end the meeting on time. Finally, give all staff an opportunity to identify ways that they think might improve the meeting process by saying what went well and what they think could use improvement.

An experiment by Bluedorn (2002) compared decisions made by more than 50 groups where participants stood up during short meetings to those made by more than 50 groups where participants sat down. Stand-up groups spent 34 percent less time and made just as many high quality decisions as the sit-down groups. Although I am not advocating that all meetings be conducted this way, be serious about letting your staff know both verbally and nonverbally that you are not interested in wasting their time.

CHAPTER FIVE

....

Taking Top-Notch Care of Yourself

Did you know that more heart attacks occur at 9:00 a.m. on Mondays than at any other time? This tells me that while cholesterol, weight, blood pressure, amount of exercise, and diet are important factors adding to risk of heart attack, job satisfaction or lack thereof may be the most important factor. While we may not always be able to control the amount of happiness we feel or the degree of meaning or purpose we get from our job, it is well-known that our thoughts and feelings influence behavior. For example, if we are depressed (feeling), we might sleep more (behavior). If we have a pleasant thought, we are more likely to smile. Victor Frankl wrote about how he survived the horrific conditions of the concentration camp by helping others, teaching others how to help each other, and focusing his thoughts on playing the piano and seeing his family again. How we think can exert a powerful influence on how we feel and what we do.

Equally true, behavior can influence thoughts and feelings. I recall driving my daughter and her friend Katie to the mall when they were about 12 years old. They were both in dreary moods. After listening to a bunch of complaints about the kinds of things that bother pubescent girls, I suggested we change the mood and laugh. They both thought this was ridiculous, but undeterred, I began forcing a laugh from the pit of my stomach. At first, they looked at me as if I needed to be locked up. But after several seconds, the forced laugh became real, spontaneous, and contagious. They both started laughing in response to my laughing, and before long we were all laughing uncontrollably. Needless to say, the mood changed dramatically. Although I rarely see her now, whenever she comes to visit, Katie jokingly asks if we can "do a laugh." Research has clearly shown that various chemicals in our brain known as neurotransmitters, such as serotonin and norepinephrine, affect our moods (Stahl, 2008) and are directly affected by how we behave (McKay, Davis, & Fanning, 2007). More on this later in the chapter.

Take Care of Yourself to Improve Your Teaching

There is mounting evidence that teachers who behave in ways that promote their own personal and professional well-being perform better in the classroom and effect better student outcomes (Duckworth, Quinn, & Seligman, 2009). Klusmann, Kunter, Trautwein, Ludtke, and Baumert (2008) found that teachers' occupational well-being and quality of instruction were enhanced by practicing "self-regulatory" behaviors (e.g., deep breathing, positive thinking). There are many things you can do to benefit your health and attitude that do not require changes in your environment or in the ways other people treat you. These strategies involve modifying the ways you think, feel, and behave. Within the last 20 years, great strides have been made in the acceptance of methods that were at one time scorned and quickly dismissed. Yet, to this day, it is rare for educators to teach simple calming strategies to their students, despite growing evidence of the benefits these techniques can have on learning and behavior. By contrast, wellness classes at the spa that teach mind-calming physical exercises and meditative mental activities are teeming with stressed out adults seeking a feeling of peacefulness and a sense of higher meaning to life beyond the mundane. In fact, Herbert Benson, who turned the medical community upside down 35 years ago by showing how simple relaxation techniques could be used to treat a host of stress-related medical disorders, found that people can influence their genes by using some of these same simple strategies (Benson & Proctor, 2010). I recently read a quote from an unknown source that said, "Meditation is a way to feel narcissistic without hurting anyone." Sounds like a good anti-depressant without the pill.

Below are some examples of activities you can do for yourself and share with your kids that can produce a sense of mindfulness and reawaken feelings of optimism. Some of this may sound "new age," "touchy-feely," and obvious. But if we can make time to shop, pay our bills, wax our eyebrows, get a physical exam, and consult with our financial planner, we can certainly plan some wellness time for ourselves and our students. Many of the activities create pleasant sensations and a feeling of calm. Some are simply fun to do. The need for fun is as basic as the need to belong and the need for sleep. Even if you don't feel like it at first, try these methods anyway. Beverly Sills, the great opera singer whose daughter was born deaf, was once asked how she dealt with that and other disappointments. She said, "I smile on the outside, hoping the inside gets the message." To gain benefit from these strategies, you must do them repeatedly before your "inside" gets the message.

Attitude Adjustment Activities

This too will probably pass

Most things in education have their day. A new superintendent arrives and wants to leave his mark on the district, so he stirs things up and brings in three new programs. Three years later, he's gone and another superintendent arrives. The latest behavior program comes along, requiring everyone to put check marks on chalk boards until it is realized that this is not the holy grail and is replaced by another program that makes everyone flip the green card to yellow and then to red. Last year's 2nd grade class was great, but this year's is the class from hell. Whole language replaces phonics and then phonics replaces whole language.

Most new programs are simply old programs with new names. When you are frustrated, try asking whether your frustration is individual or system-based. Is it being caused by specific things that are happening right now but not likely to continue forever, or are these systemic issues that are indigenous to working in schools? There will always be one or a few difficult kids, challenging parents, insensitive administrators, and stupid policies. Quitting or changing your environment is probably best when you are continually complaining about many of these factors or about a few big ones over a long period of time. Continuous exposure to negative factors and events that affect you and over which you have little or no control is unhealthy. Otherwise, recognize that what is going on is probably going to change sooner or later, and is probably not worth your continued worry.

> *Suggestion:* The next time you feel frustrated, write down all of the things that are contributing to your frustration. Look at your list and put an asterisk next to anything that has been ongoing with no end in sight. This will exclude many items like "my class is driving me crazy," because the year will eventually end and you will have a new class. For whatever remains, put a C next to anything over which you have some or a lot of control (like how and what I teach when my door is closed) or an N next to those items over which you have little or no control (like what is going to be on the state exam). What is your plan to improve your Cs? What can you do to not let the Ns get to you as much as they are right now? If you care about your kids and know you are a good teacher, don't change your dream, change your strategy.

Be thankful every day for at least three consecutive weeks

I know it sounds corny but appreciate how lucky you are in comparison to so many other people. I was recently inspired by an article I read in my local newspaper, the *Rochester Democrat and Chronicle* (Swingle, 2011), about Bret Hoefen, a 32-year-old man with a rare, life-threatening form of cancer. He has a tattoo on his right arm that reads "Today is my best day," and he explains "It means tomorrow I won't be as healthy as I am today." On his left arm another tattoo says, "Ride in a good direction," meaning "keep searching out interesting, exciting things to do." Like many of us, before he had his diagnosis, he and his wife were living routine lives and planning for their futures; he was working and pursuing an MBA; she had a job at the local university. They put off having children until after finishing their graduate degrees and were saving some money. After his diagnosis, Bret and his wife bought motorcycles and a trailer and set out with his parents to see the country and savor life. He plans to stay on the road until either the money runs out or he is too sick to continue. Bret writes a daily blog about his experiences and relishes sharing it. He says, "Whatever happens, this makes me feel like, up to the last minute, I can be creating something."

On a recent trip to Eastern Europe, I sadly had too many moments to appreciate the richness of my life as I visited the horror of the millions herded to their deaths at the Holocaust concentration camps in Poland. Remind yourself every day that as challenging as life might get in the classroom or at school, neither you nor your students are in a hospital battling for your lives or in an abjectly poor village without fresh water.

> *Suggestion:* Keep a "Three Good Things Journal" to record three things that go well each day and what you think caused each positive event. Research has shown that people who do this activity for one week report fewer symptoms of depression and higher levels of happi-

ness for six months. Those who continued to keep track longer showed the strongest long-term gains in happiness (Seligman, Steen, Park, & Peterson, 2005).

Every day, express gratitude for "negatives"

When I get down, I find it healthy to wallow in the misery for a while, but then it is better to get out of the muck. This is best accomplished by reminding myself of the many things for which I am grateful. So may I suggest that you throw your own pity party for the next short while, get it out of your system, and then take stock of all the things and people around you, including the "negative" things that have happened to make you a better and stronger person. Diane Trim (2010) of Magna Publications thanked me in a recent article from that organization for inspiring her to be thankful for her *challenging students*. A few of the things she wrote:

Luke and Ian: Thank you for teaching me that I need to be very calm with some students. Keeping my voice steady and low when you push my buttons helps to prevent the situation from escalating.

Chris and Joel: I let your antics control my class. You taught me how to deal with students who take over. It was a valuable classroom management lesson. I've never forgotten it, and I am better for it.

Kurt: I tried everything to get you to put pen to paper. Who knew it would be poetry that did the trick? You taught me that a small amount of success can really help a student turn a corner. Thank you.

I'll share a few of my own:

Ben (program developer): I apologize for all the people who blamed you for the failure of the parenting program we ran together. It taught me two important lessons early in my career: great ideas aren't enough and blaming others is usually a cover for cowardly fear.

John (principal): Thanks for converting the storage closet to make me an office. I learned early on that my space was far less important than my sensitivity in connecting with students and teachers.

Bill (student): Bill, you are a strong-willed person with a mind of your own. Even though we sometimes get into it with each other, I have a lot of respect for how you stand up for what you think is right.

Now it is your turn. Identify challenging people or difficult events that have made you stronger and for which you are thankful. Write a note addressed to them that you may or may not send that tells them how their presence or why the event makes you a stronger person. Finally, consider sending your note or expressing these sentiments verbally.

Be your own best friend

When you regret something you said or did, you can virtually always do something to redeem yourself, but it is first necessary to forgive yourself. What do you say or do to help your friends when they make mistakes, get mad at themselves, are having a bad day, or have a problem that they share with you? Most friends say or do things like:

- You'll do better next time.
- Everybody makes mistakes.
- Nobody is perfect.
- Wow, what a bummer.
- I don't always do my best either.
- Don't worry about it.
- Let's talk about it.
- I'm here for you.
- I understand.
- Give a hug or change the topic to a more pleasant one.

Some friends might even give a little gift or write a thoughtful note of reassurance. What are some other things that friends do for each other when things aren't going well or they are feeling bad?

- _____
- _____
- _____
- _____

> *Suggestion:* How about saying or doing some of these things to or for yourself when things aren't going right for you? You are the most important person there is, and you deserve to be at least as good to yourself as you might be to others. It is very important to be kind to yourself when things aren't going well. None of us are perfect, and we all do things that we feel sorry about. You will be better able to figure out how to change things after you forgive yourself. Just as you would say or do things to cheer up a friend, do the same for yourself. Try to live by the reverse of the familiar motto "Do unto others as you would have them do unto you." Instead, *Do for yourself as you usually do for others.*

Do your best, but then turn the page

Faulty advice I often hear parents and teachers give kids is to work hard at everything they do. "Try your best!" is an exhortation often exclaimed by parents, teachers, and coaches. It is important to have a good work ethic, but at everything? Does "try your best" mean your best for that moment or that day or based on the mood you are experiencing right then or the best you could ever do on your best day? What if it isn't your best day? What if the conditions "on the field" are far less than ideal? Perhaps better advice would be to work hard and try your best at things that matter to you while you are doing them—but when the game is over, turn the page. It seems to me that people who are compelled to work hard and who are constantly trying their best can easily become perfectionists who experience little joy in what they do.

A good example for me is golf. When I first started playing golf, I stunk, but I enjoyed being out on the course. Walking the course made me feel relaxed, and although I really liked hitting a good shot, how I scored didn't really matter. As I began to take the game more seriously and worked at getting better, I actually started enjoying it less. The game began to feel like a burden. A Mark Twain quote sadly began to make sense: "Golf is a good walk spoiled." I felt stressed when I hit a bad shot. Anxiety would set in when I played with better golfers. Bad shots and high scores became the focus rather than having a good, relaxing time at a beautiful place. For a guy like me who has little time to practice and has no aspirations to play in the club's tournament, perhaps it is best to just play with other hackers, have fun enjoying the serenity of the surroundings, practice occasionally when I can, and not care about the score. With this renewed attitude, I recently started playing again after a long hiatus from the game.

Perhaps the best advice is to work hard at things you like to do and that you value doing, because few of us can really be good at everything. With everything else, perhaps a healthier attitude is to work as little as necessary in order to get by. Hire others to do the things you aren't good at or interested in. If you love teaching history, work hard to develop as much expertise as you can. If you hate math but have to teach it, work enough to get good enough to get by. If you love riding your bike, ride it a lot. Do less to keep your upper body toned (because bike riding won't help) unless you want to be a body builder. If you want more resources to help you do your job, lobby as many people as hard as you can with as much diplomacy as you have, but then move on. On an episode of the television show *House*, a dying patient was offering advice to one of the doctors. The doctor's philosophy was that he didn't want to have any regrets on his deathbed. The patient told him, "You shouldn't worry about how you will feel on your deathbed because you will only spend one day on it. It is all the other days you should worry about." Enjoy your journey.

Stay open to new possibilities

Great teachers are enthusiastic about new possibilities and will often find the silver lining in the cloud. Keep yourself fresh by trying new things. Nothing new is ever discovered by just staying in one's current comfort zone. Imagine how different the world would be if Thomas Edison had been sufficiently satisfied with the amount of illumination that was then offered by candles. Imagine if Beethoven or the Beatles thought all the best music had already been written.

At some point, some great teacher took a leap and experimented with the possibility that some kids could learn rules of math more easily when paired with music while others would do better leaving the basal behind and reading a sports magazine. Another teacher at some point stopped requiring a squirmy student to sit still while working and played with the idea or stumbled upon allowing that student to work at a music stand. Yet another allowed a doodling student to draw the main causes of the Civil War rather than write about them. Although these examples are still not mainstream practices, it is not unusual for at least a few teachers in most schools to adopt practices like these. I currently hear a fair number of teachers and parents complain about how video games are contributing to creating more ADHD and/or amoral kids. Yet a 2010 University of Rochester study found that playing action video games for 50 hours improved a person's ability to make fast decisions and to multitask (Green, Pouget, & Bavelier). Maybe we should be expecting students to play video games as homework! Perhaps it is a good idea to allow, or maybe even encourage, kids to play action video games on school time. Maybe *we* should be playing action video games as well! Stay open to the possibility that you might discover a new way to teach your content by pairing it with a video game. When we stay open to new possibilities, novel solutions to sticky problems often emerge. Could it be that the best methods for teaching and learning have not yet been discovered?

> *Suggestion:* Think about a school problem that increases your stress and that seems to have no satisfactory solution. For many teachers, students texting with cell phones is high on their list. At a department or faculty meeting, challenge yourself and your colleagues to think of as many ways as possible to solve this problem other than having a rule that prohibits the behavior. Because students often find ways to sabotage rules they hate, which leads to a cat-and-mouse game that adds to our stress, you might consider figuring out how allowing or redirecting the problem might either enhance learning or make teaching better for you.

Challenge yourself

Are you starting to feel stale? Does it seem like you are doing the same things over and over, and while the kids may seem fine, you are bored? Consider taking on a new challenge such as teaching a subject outside your area of certification (most states and school districts permit a limited number of classes to be taught outside a teacher's area of certification). You might feel uneasy about tackling this. It is easy to convince yourself that you don't need the hassle, stress, and bother. Why make yourself feel anxious when you can just breeze through? Because a new challenge usually awakens the juices and gets us going again. It is normal to feel anxious while taking on something new. Keep in mind that anxiety is often the springboard to excitement. Use your natural energy and curiosity to awaken your dormant creativity. If you usually teach social studies, it may be a stretch to teach science, but realize that even if you weren't the strongest science student, maybe you can teach a lower-level class.

Another possibility is to volunteer to teach a different type of student. If you currently teach advanced classes, consider teaching a lower-level class and vice versa. Sometimes we get so stuck in the same comfortable rut, we wind up dulling our senses and intellectual need for stimulation. Yet another possibility is to connect with students in a different way. Consider coaching a sport or being the faculty adviser to a club on campus. Get involved as a teacher representative negotiating a new contract with the district or join a school committee exploring who to bring in for the next staff development conference. Perhaps you might try getting involved with your school's parent-teacher organization. Is there anything you have thought would be cool to do, but to this point you have dismissed it because you either think of the task as difficult or yourself as unqualified? Embracing this possibility might trigger anxiety and uncertainty, but is also likely to awaken you. See where it takes you.

> *Suggestion:* Awakening the juices requires taking action. What words come to mind that characterize a new challenge? For most people, a new challenge means participating in ventures that require one or more of the following: *creating, planning, developing, implementing, supervising, overseeing, organizing, managing, launching, evaluating, serving on, working with.* Are there others? What "ventures" might be open or available in your class, school, or district that tap the words you listed? For example:
>
> • *Implementing* the new experimental social studies curriculum.
> • *Working with* administration on the new discipline policy.
> • *Supervising* a student teacher.
> • *Organizing* a community service project with students.
> • *Planning* ways to make lessons have more fun.
> • *Serving on* the union's negotiating committee.
>
> Now make your own list. Afterward, rank your items from most interesting to least interesting and then take action.

Mental and Emotional Activities

Make time to laugh

The health benefits of laughter at both a physiological and emotional level are indisputable. Although few disagree with laughter's benefits, many believe that you first have to feel happy in order to laugh. Well, if you are in a classroom or school with inadequate resources, you may not feel like laughing. So schedule times for laughter and then laugh during those times whether you feel like it or not! Let's face it: you and your kids need and deserve some fun, especially when the surroundings provide little reason to laugh.

As already noted, various studies have linked laughter to a boost in endorphins which is known to lower stress, prevent heart disease, diminish pain, and improve resistance to disease (Scott, 2011). There is little doubt that laughter impacts brain chemistry in a positive way and very likely improves the brain's ability to entertain new information. Emotional benefits include improved mood, increased joy, and less anxiety. It is virtually impossible to feel sad, depressed, unhappy, angry, or stressed when laughing. In fact, roaring laughter is probably more contagious than the common cold. Laughter can also help defuse conflict, enhance teamwork, and strengthen relationships. To those of you who are already comfortable letting yourself loose with laughter, keep it up. In fact, let it spread. Most other people will enjoy being around you. You will influence the mood at your school and in your classroom in a positive way. If you are not accustomed to laughing because it has not been a natural part of your life until now, start by setting aside special times to seek humor. One of the best things you can do is hang out with or watch somebody who you think is funny. Read the comics, watch a sitcom, go to a funny movie, listen to a comedian, goof around with kids, or make funny noises with your dog. It can be helpful to have these experiences so that when your scheduled laugh times at school arrive, you will have some humorous images you can recapture to start the process.

Consider starting a laughter club at your school or in your community, or join one that already exists. Silly as it might sound, there are more than 6,000 clubs in more than 60 countries (including the United States) where people gather to laugh. This practice was begun by Dr. Madan Kataria, a physician in India popularly known as the "Guru of Giggling," as he was researching the medical benefits of laughter. The idea quickly spread. Typically, those at clubs get into a basic standing or seated yoga position (such as hands and head held high), and they laugh continuously for several minutes. Movement often accompanies the laughter. No jokes are told.

Because laughter starts with a smile, practice smiling. What is funny to you? What makes you laugh? Be sure to keep a smile on your face for at least 10-second intervals. Try it now. How do you feel? Now exaggerate the smile. Show more teeth. It might help for you to think of something funny that has happened in the past that made you smile from your teeth to your toes. Very slowly let that smile move through your throat and into your stomach. Notice how you might even want to start laughing. Laughing all the way from deep down in your stomach up through your chest and out your mouth is one of the best things you can do to feel good. Give yourself permission. Try this several times a day. In fact, the next time you are in a grouchy mood, whether at home, at school, or at a family visit, try smiling and let it grow. Even bearing your teeth in a forced grin will provide benefit. Your brain releases endorphins when you smile, whether you mean it or not.

Practice mindfulness

When I was healing from my hip replacement surgery a few years ago, I was largely incapacitated and dependent upon others to assist me with basic things for an extended period of time. On a day-to-day basis, I had to fight feeling frustrated at the slowness of healing. The many technological advances that we take for granted have led to impatience when we don't get what we are seeking immediately. This applies to virtually everything: waiting too long for our food to arrive at a restaurant or for the computer to boot up; waiting in snarled traffic; waiting for the plane to take off; waiting for our child to get ready to go; waiting for a student to come on time or care about the class. It is easy to transform from a kind, thoughtful person to a mean, angry, tense ogre in a matter of a few seconds.

One solution is to practice mindfulness. It means paying attention on purpose to what is happening to you in the moment both inside and outside your skin. It means paying attention to all the sensations of even basic tasks like breathing (noticing the movement of your chest and diaphragm when you breathe), moving (feeling sensations as you move), and listening (directing your attention to a focus on the sounds around you). Being mindful means paying attention to the experience you are having without trying to change it. At its fullest, being a mindful person is about embracing the full range of your sensations, feelings, and outside experiences. It means being with the kid who is struggling and resonating to his feelings rather than trying to get him to change. It means taking deep breaths and being thankful that we can. Most of the strategies that follow will help you develop or refine your mindfulness so that you feel more relaxed, refreshed, and attuned to your surroundings.

> *Suggestion:* Take some time today to notice small things that often escape your attention. Focus on the aromas around you like the coffee brewing and the donuts baking. Close your eyes and feel the sensation of massage on your back as you shower. Notice how your feet meet the carpet as you walk barefoot through your house. Pay attention to a happy smiling face of one of your kids or the

hunched shoulders with head bowed of another. Try to stay with each moment and allow yourself to fluidly move on to the next. Notice how you feel. Is there anything you want to say or do?

Practice being mindful of others

One day I was with my adult son who is in business with me and we had a conflict that bothered me. When we began working together, my money funded the business. Over time, he has assumed ownership and a few days earlier had repaid my money. As we were discussing a business issue that we have a difference of opinion over, he became upset with me and in my view emotionally aroused in a way that was disproportionate to the issue. Instead of focusing on his feelings and trying to defuse the situation, I became upset. One comment led to another and eventually to a shouting match. Realizing nothing good was going to happen if this continued, I left. After calming down shortly thereafter, a light bulb went off in my head. My focus turned to how I had contributed to the incident. What could I have done differently? I realized that I had missed what was most important to him. I hadn't listened to him. Rather than getting outside myself to focus on him, I had been too entrenched in my position. He had just repaid a loan and was feeling proud of that accomplishment. It was symbolic of his success, and I believe he wanted to celebrate that seminal moment with his dad. His was the pain of a son feeling ignored by his father at a moment of achievement.

By contrast, in my mind, he was repaying a loan, which is what ethical people should do and therefore not especially worthy of praise and appreciation. Because we might not always recognize a moment of importance to somebody else, make it a point to say or do something appreciative when someone does something thoughtful. Don't take it or them for granted. When we are with other people, being mindful is about what is happening to them as well as to you. Join their experience, for to miss it can easily turn mindfulness into selfishness.

It seems like human nature to take for granted the many positive things that happen every day. Get into the habit of appreciating the little things. Is there someone in your class, school, or life right now that you see as angry or mean? What does that person do that you find annoying? What is your best guess about what he or she is seeking? Do you think this person feels fulfilled or dismissed? Noticed or ignored? What do you or others do when this person is *not* behaving in an annoying way? Consider the possibility that this person's annoying behavior simply represents frustration about wanting appreciation, attention, or notice and not getting it. Is it possible that you miss some things about this person that are worthy of notice in a positive way? Make a list of all the things that could be seen as positive. You might have to "stretch." (For example: She is always brave enough to voice her opinion. As annoying as she is, there is no doubt she feels deeply about her kids). Now that you have at least a few positives, make a regular habit of initiating a friendly comment to him or her based upon what you identified. You might begin to get a different reaction from this person, but even if you don't, be one of those people at school who finds a way to take the high road.

Stay with the feeling

It is natural to want to push away negative feelings like anger, disgust, boredom, fear, and unhappiness. Some years ago, I began experiencing anxiety or panic attacks that would appear unexpectedly and last for a while. Out of nowhere, my heart would begin to race, I would have trouble breathing, my mouth would be dry, and I would feel light-headed. I was convinced that I was having a heart attack, no doubt in part reinforced by the fact that my father had suddenly died from cardiac arrest at a young age. All medical tests showed that my heart and other key organs were fine, leading to the conclusion that the culprit was anxiety. Not a big fan of anti-anxiety medication at the time, I checked in with a therapist who was helpful to some degree, but the panic attacks continued. The breakthrough came one day while I was jogging and feeling good, but then suddenly my peacefulness was interrupted by these dreaded symptoms. I think out of sheer disgust and frustration, I decided right then that I was going to keep on jogging no matter what. I had had everything checked out medically, and they kept telling me my heart was okay. If I died, I died. I just wasn't going to worry about dying any longer. I remember looking up at the bright blue sunny sky with this new determination to just let whatever was going to happen, happen. And to my surprise and relief, the symptoms of anxiety morphed into excitement and joy. There I was, running carefree, feeling at one with the world around me.

I have found that most of us want to avoid feeling whatever bothersome emotion we have, yet the key to moving on is to step into the emotion rather than running away from it. Let yourself feel whatever is going on. If you are feeling annoyed, bothered, sad, overwhelmed, or agitated, stay with it. Be miserable. In fact, exaggerate the misery. You might even consider taking a day off and throwing yourself a "misery party" where you just allow yourself to feel the depth of your misery from head to toe. Give the emotion a voice. What does it want to say? In the privacy of your car ride home or when nobody is around in your classroom, try to picture whatever is bothering you and tell that to the person or the situation with as much fervor as you feel. Then switch roles and answer back. Keep the inner dialogue going until you finish. After you have emptied yourself, some other thought, emotion, or insight will emerge. That will allow you to really move on.

Have a selfless buddy

For most teachers, even great ones, there is little overt daily appreciation for what we do. Most of us receive little notice, recognition, respect, and in many cases money. Resentment can set in and we may lose focus on what is really most important. Envy and jealousy may interfere with collaboration and collegiality when another teacher's class gets higher test scores or someone else receives a thank-you card from a parent or is nominated to be teacher of the year. Being a great teacher requires selfless devotion to your students whether you are recognized or not. Yet none of us is perfect, and it is not always easy to look in the mirror and see ourselves objectively. To stay focused, it can be very helpful to pair up with a colleague or friend who you trust and who can tell it like it is. Use this person regularly to put a check on yourself to ensure that ego does not get in the way of humility. As my wife Barbara, who taught for 30 years (the last 10 of them mentoring other teachers), always said about one issue or another, "It is about the kids. How will this make life better for the kids?" Winning awards, getting nice notes from parents, and receiving recognition from the principal is nice, but do you really need these things to make life better for your kids? Isn't your life better when your students' lives get better? Get together with your buddy to make sure you are keeping the emphasis where it needs to be and are not getting lured into gossip or motivated by envy.

Use positive self-talk

When you hear your students using negative thinking with words like "I can't," "I'm unable," or "It's too hard," encourage them to add the word "yet" or "so far." Do the same thing for yourself. When you think you can't ever achieve something, you lose hope. Make your challenges temporary and teach kids to do the same. Remind yourself and teach your students that most of the conversations we have each day are with ourselves. Pick a day and check it out. How you talk to yourself affects the decisions you make. Telling yourself that talking to the principal for more support is useless because you've done it twice before and it hasn't worked won't give you the support you are seeking. You have a better chance by thinking, "I'll talk to him one more time and give the best reason I can. If it doesn't work, I'll check with a few other teachers and see if there are some ideas I can get from them that might make things better." It isn't very helpful for a student who does poorly on a test to think, "I am really stupid." It would be much more helpful for him to think, "I'll need to work harder, practice more, and ask for help from somebody who is better at this than I am." When talking about positive self-talk with your students, give them a few more situations to help them see how their thoughts affect how they feel. Which way is it better to think?

1. "My parents are getting divorced. If I was better, I bet they would have stayed together." Or "My parents are getting divorced, but kids can't control what grown-ups do. I feel sad and scared, but I know it is not my fault."

2. "Nobody picked me to be a partner because nobody likes me." Or "I wasn't picked this time, so I'll work alone and I'll pick a partner next time."

3. "Writing is hard for me, so I guess I just won't do the work." Or "Writing is hard for me, so I will need to spend more time doing the work even though I'd rather be doing other things."

4. "That was a stupid test. I studied hard, but my teacher asked stupid questions. Oh well." Or "That was a tough test and now I know the kinds of questions my teacher asks. I'll have to study those kinds of questions for the next test."

Now try the same thing with situations you currently face that are stressing you out.

1. What is the situation? (For example, parent complains endlessly about everything I do.)

2. Thinking that is not helpful: "She's a jerk." "No wonder this kid has problems." "Maybe I am a bad teacher."

3. What I could tell myself: "Most parents don't complain about me, and even she only complains twice a week. She's a

misguided but concerned parent. Even though she is difficult, maybe I can guide her or learn from her."

4. When you are feeling stressed or locked into negative thinking, practice talking to yourself in a more helpful way.

A potpourri of rapid relaxants

Most educators both need and deserve momentary breaks from the variety of stressors we face virtually every day. There are several strategies you can use that take very little time to get yourself refocused, re-energized, and revitalized.

1. Think of some calming words (i.e., *calm, peaceful, soothing, relaxed*). Pick one and slowly repeat the word to yourself for a few minutes with your eyes open or closed (Note: This alone is a good activity, but it can also be paired with the next one for an even better result).

2. Picture a time in your life when the problem that is bothering you was not present. Try to step into that picture and stay there for at least the next few minutes.

3. Take a few minutes in the morning and then again in the afternoon and stare out the window, sending all your thoughts and worries away.

4. Play music that you like at the beginning and end of class, and sometimes in the background while you are teaching.

5. Watch a funny DVD during lunch or break.

6. Close your eyes and cover them with the palms of your hands for one minute. Do this at least a few times every day.

7. Whistle or hum a tune you like while you walk through the halls, cafeteria, and from room to room.

8. When you might start thinking in some situation, "OH NO!" substitute quietly saying, "WOW."

9. Remember that people and technology can be imperfect, just as you are sometimes.

10. Remind yourself that if what you are concerned about won't matter six months or a year from now, it's probably not that important in the overall picture.

11. Have a worries wastebasket. If and when you find yourself obsessing over something you can no longer control or something from the past that you can't relive, write down the worry and place it in a special wastebasket. When you are really ready to let go, say your good-byes and dump the wastebasket in the trash.

Physical Activities

The following activities require some alone time where you won't be disturbed for at least 10 minutes. They are therefore 10-Minutes-or-Less Stress Busters.

Squeeze and release

1. Sit up straight in a comfortable chair with your hands in your lap and your feet on the floor. Be away from everyone. It is best to close your eyes.

2. Tense, tighten, or squeeze the muscles in your feet, legs, and toes as tightly as you can while silently counting to five. Release and repeat.

3. Now do the same with your chest and stomach. Tighten up those muscles as you silently count to five, then release.

4. Go to your arms, fingers, and shoulders. Tighten up these muscles. Silently count to five, then let go. Feel the relaxation. Repeat.

5. Now go to your head and neck. Scrunch up the muscles of your face as you count to five, then relax those muscles. Do it again and make sure that you scrunch your mouth, nose, and eyes, each time counting to five before relaxing.

Now go back to your feet and do the same thing again. Squeeze or tighten each body part, count to five, then relax. When you finish, open your eyes and notice how calm your whole body feels.

Empty chair

1. Sit in a chair and place an empty chair across from you so that you are looking right at it.

2. Picture a difficult student, parent, or colleague who is making you feel angry, sad, or upset seated in the empty chair.

3. Tell the person in the chair what he or she says or does that bothers you. Don't hold back.

4. When you are finished, switch chairs. Imagine yourself as this other person and respond to what you have heard. In addition, tell "yourself" in the other empty chair whatever might be going on that is bothering you (this will require you to take the perspective of the person).

5. Keep switching back and forth until both sides have finished speaking.

6. Now that you have told this person in the chair your gripes, think about what (if anything) you might really want to say the next time you get a chance.

Letting go

These four strategies are immediate ways to release tension:

Towel twisting is a way for the hands to release tension. Keep a towel in your desk. If you feel tense, twist the towel as if it is full of water and needs to be wrung out. If there are specific individuals that easily come to mind, imagine that they are the towel and "wring" them out.

Towel biting lets the tension out of your mouth. If you notice yourself holding in your tension or anger by biting down hard against your own teeth, try biting as hard as you want on the towel. As with towel twisting, if there are specific individuals that come to mind, "bite" them!

Opening your mouth as wide as you can without straining and keeping it open to the count of five is a good stress buster. Then close until your teeth touch to the count of five. Do this five times. Next, open your mouth and transfer the energy so that all the muscles in your mouth are tilted to the right side of your mouth. Be sure to feel the muscles in the right side of your neck and upper shoulder, as well as your right eye, contract as you open your mouth. Keep it open and stretched to the count of five. Now do the same thing on the left side. Repeat a few times.

Silently screaming is another stress buster. Scream without straining your vocal cords. There will probably be a quiet "H" as you exhale. Screams are virtually always accompanied by body movement, so let as many other parts of your body get involved as you want.

Make room for exercise

There is already a substantial amount of information that touts the health benefits of exercise for both children and adults. Most who exercise report feeling rejuvenated and relaxed following their workouts. Although I have been advocating exercise as a means to improve both academics and behavior with students for a long time, until recently there was little formal research on this subject. That has changed.

There is now considerable research data showing the multi-dimensional benefits of physical activity in schools. Increased physical activity has been associated with better physical health (Burton & VanHeest, 2007), improved mental health (Floriani & Kennedy, 2008), and higher academic achievement (Tompo-rowski, Davis, Miller, & Naglieri, 2008). After periods of physical activity, kids with impulse control problems and inattentiveness (which are hallmarks of ADHD) exhibit greater on-task behaviors that include completion of required assignments (Gapin & Etnier, 2009; Shepard, 1997). Physical exercise has been found to be as effective as drug treatment and psychotherapy in the treatment of childhood depression (Craft & Perna, 2004; Lawlor & Hopkins, 2001); obsessive compulsive disorders (Abrantes et al., 2009), aggression (Allison, Basile, & MacDonald, 1991) and disruptive behavior (Bachman & Sluyter, 1988) were all decreased through the use of physical exercise. Even the self-stimulatory behavior of children with autism was found to decrease while at the same time academic performance increased with mildly strenuous aerobic activity (Celiberti, Bobo, Kelly, Harris, & Handelman, 1997; Elliott, Dobbin, Rose, & Soper, 1994, Rosenthal-Malek & Mitchell, 1997). Symptoms of PTSD were dramatically reduced among female teenagers who briskly walked 1.5 miles within 23 minutes after a one-minute warm-up of slow walking and a one-minute cool down following exercise three times a week over five weeks (Diaz & Motta, 2008).

Although there hasn't been any research to date that specifically looks at potential benefits like these for teachers, it seems logical to think that teachers could achieve similar benefits to those achieved by students. But even if that isn't the case, there is no down side to increasing your physical activity in accordance with your health status. If you aren't already doing so, consider a more extensive program of exercise outside of school. At school, consider doing very brief exercises when you have a few minutes. Naturally, if you have some physical limitations, check with your health care provider first. Here are some possibilities:

Toe lifts. While standing, reach up toward the ceiling while balancing on the tips of your toes. Raise and lower 10 times. Pause for a moment and repeat four or five times.

March in place. For two to three minutes, march in place as if you are in a marching band, lifting each leg high off the ground.

Run in place. Same as above except run instead of march.

Briskly walk back and forth. In between classes or during a free period, briskly walk through the halls.

Do steps. Climb up and down a set of steps (try for at least a 10-step incline). Keep doing this until you begin to feel winded. Increase gradually.

Standing push-ups. Stand facing an empty wall. Extend both arms outward chest high until your arms are perpendicular to your body with the palms of your hands touching the wall. Keep your feet still and push forward and backward with your hands against the wall for several repetitions. As you feel stronger, move just a little farther back so that you have to be on the tips of your toes to reach the wall with the palms of your hands.

Hand pushing. Either seated or standing, place the palms of your hands out in front of you in a "praying" position with all parts of each hand touching the other. Breathe in to the count of five keeping your hands lightly touching. As you exhale, push your hands together as hard as you can to the count of five.

Head rolls. Do a few shoulder and head rolls in all directions.

⑦ Questions for Reflection

1. Sustaining greatness as a teacher means taking good care of yourself physically, emotionally, and for many, spiritually. What are you currently doing for yourself in each of these domains? What else might you do?

2. When you are faced with challenges in your life outside of school, what do you usually do to muster up the effort to get the job done? Can you see any ways to apply strategies you typically use outside of school to make yourself feel more fulfilled at school?

3. Research points to the benefits of exercise and calming strategies for improvement in learning and behavior among challenging students. Have you explored, developed, or implemented programs of exercise or mental relaxation with them? What have you found? What are some ways you can think of to incorporate exercise or mental relaxation into the curriculum?

4. Who might you further consult to help you develop or refine physical, emotional, or spiritual strategies for yourself and/or your students?

5. Sustaining greatness is about keeping yourself inspired and inspiring others. Who or what does that for you in or out of school? Consider seeking more of this when your batteries are in need of a recharge.

Key Chapter Thoughts

- There is mounting evidence that teachers who behave in ways that promote their own personal and professional well-being perform better and get better student outcomes.
- Remind yourself every day that as challenging as life might get in the classroom or at school, neither you nor your students are in a hospital battling for your lives or in an abjectly poor village without fresh water.
- It seems like human nature to take for granted the many positive things that happen every day. Get into the habit of appreciating the little things.
- Great teachers are enthusiastic about new possibilities and will often find the silver lining in the cloud. Keep yourself fresh by trying new things.
- Increased physical activity has been associated with better physical health, improved mental health, and higher academic achievement.
- Make room for laughter every day. It will make you a better teacher and a happier person.

For the Administrator

It is well known that teaching is one of the most stressful occupations. Because the vast majority of teachers really care about the kids they see every day, it is easy for them to feel overwhelmed by the many needs their students have and the limited capacity to help most of them in meaningful ways. I think it is fair to say that being a school administrator is no less stressful. You have less direct contact with students, so you are likely to have even less direct influence on the lives of your students. While you are the most important person when it comes to setting the tone at school, rarely do you have a lot of say when it comes to district or state policy that nowadays attempts to cover everything from what students are expected to learn to how much space per square foot is required for each student. If you are running a top-notch school, it is probably as much in spite of the policies you are expected to enforce as because of them. You have probably figured out some good ways to protect your faculty and students from being affected by the full force of nutty policies, standards, and expectations. You will much more often get everyone's complaints, gripes, problems, and blame than credit for their successes. It just seems to be the nature of the job. So my hope is that you experience as much benefit from the strategies in this section as your teachers do because you must take good care of yourself if you are to be the positive force at your school that is so needed for your teachers. And if anyone is underappreciated, it is most likely to be you because you are usually behind the scenes planning for the successes and giving credit to others when success is recognized.

One of the more difficult challenges you might face as an administrator is dealing with teachers whose job performance is suffering due to personal issues that you may or may not know about. I have found the best way is to be caring and honest as you express your concerns, with the goal of having teachers seek the help they need to get better. You might say something like, "Jill, I'm noticing lately that you seem more tense and stressed out than usual. What is going on?" If there is denial, gently push on by describing specific instances of behavior that are out of character.

("I know Joey can be difficult, but reaming him out the way you did is not like you. It's also not like you to miss a faculty meeting and arrive late to school. You know how much I respect you, and I only want to help.") While some people find it difficult to open up, most will appreciate the concern.

The great news is that you have total control within your school when it comes to being a proponent of the kinds of strategies described in this section. You can either legitimize these methods or dismiss them. And despite all of the research that shows the emotional benefits to adults and the behavioral and academic benefits to students of deep breathing, meditation, guided visualization, and related strategies, these practices still remain on the fringe, if anywhere, in most schools. Yet when teachers as citizens join their spa or health club, these are mainstream methods. Be courageous and bring the real world to your school. Not only is it wise to encourage your faculty to practice these techniques on their own time, make yourself cutting-edge by weaving these methods into the fabric of your school. Use time at faculty meetings to learn and practice. Meet with your mental health professionals who are often versed in wellness strategies and explore what and how to best share these with staff. Consider forming an after-school club for brisk walking. It might even be worth your while to invest in a treadmill, exercise bike, and elliptical machine for staff use, especially if a shower is available. Twenty minutes on the machine and a 10-minute shower during a free period still leaves some time for a cup of coffee.

Conclusion

Keeping teachers at the top of their game means staying focused on what really matters: making a positive difference in the lives of students. The more we enrich their lives, the more satisfied we are. They need our A-game every day. While realistically not every day will be as good as the one before or after, it is never okay for us to be satisfied with a "bad day."

I recently ran into Pat, a 30-something man at the local supermarket who had been one of my students from years ago. I first met him when he was in 3rd grade at an elementary school where I had been a school psychologist and he was a troubled and troubling boy. Pat had a knack for driving his teachers crazy, so we tried diligently year after year to place him with as many teachers as we could who were good in working with difficult students. When I asked what he was doing these days, he told me that he was visiting his mom but was working out of town. After drifting through a few jobs, he had gone back to school part-time and had become a teacher. I nearly fell over! He was now working with tough high school kids and loving it. No wonder, because he probably knew what they had up their sleeves before they did. When I asked why he became a teacher, he reminded me of those teachers that he had when he was a kid who refused to give up on him. In particular, he singled out Ms. C., a no-nonsense yet deeply caring teacher he had in high school who was instrumental in getting him to see himself as capable and talented. He told me about a time after he had "lost it" that she had taken him aside. Though he was expecting a scolding, she instead told him how important he was to her, how smart he was, what a leader he had become, and how successful she knew he was going to be. Although she knew his limitations as a struggling reader, she assured him that he already had plenty going for him and with her help, he could get better academically. Pat made it clear that it was because of Ms. C. and a few of his other teachers that he was able to see and take a different path in life.

In order to develop into a fulfilled, productive adult, every Pat needs at least one important, respected individual who sees his worth before he sees his own. All students need at least an occasional "aha" moment where they finally master the concept or see the world in a slightly different way. Staying on top of our game is about having passion, energy, and belief in our students even when they have little belief or confidence in themselves. While it can be easy to get distracted or frustrated by poor behavior, uncooperative and unappreciative adults, and inadequate resources, keep the focus on what is most important. Every day we get an opportunity with a captive audience to expand the world for them and make a difference in their lives. On their behalf, I want to thank you for bringing your A-game every day, especially when teaching gets tough!

References

Abrantes, A. M., Strong, D. R., Cohn, A., Cameron, A. Y., Greenberg, B. D., Mancebo, M. C., et al. (2009). Acute changes in obsessions and compulsions following moderate-intensity aerobic exercise among patients with obsessive compulsive disorder. *Journal of Anxiety Disorders, 23*, 923–927.

Allison, D. B., Basile, V. C. & MacDonald, R. B. (1991). Brief report: Comparative effects of antecedent exercise and lorazepam on the aggressive behavior of an autistic man. *Journal of Autism and Developmental Disorders, 21*, 89–94.

Bachman, J. E., & Sluyter, D. (1988). Reducing inappropriate behaviors of developmentally disabled adults using antecedent aerobic dance exercises. *Research in Developmental Disabilities, 9*, 73–83.

Benson, H. & Proctor, W. (2010). *Relaxation revolution: Enhancing your personal health through the science & genetics of mind body healing.* New York: Scribner.

Bluedorn, A. C. (2002). *The human organization of time: Temporal realities and experience.* Palo Alto, CA: Stanford University Press.

Buckingham, M. (2005). *The one thing you need to know.* New York: Free Press.

Burton, L. J., & VanHeest, J. L. (2007). The importance of physical activity in closing the achievement gap. *Quest, 59*, 212–218.

Bushman, C. J., Moeller, S. J., & Crocker, J. (2010). Sweets, sex or self-esteem? Comparing the value of self-esteem boosts with other pleasant rewards. *Journal of Personality.* Accepted Article. doi: 10.1111/j. 1467-6494.2010.00712.x.

Carver, C. L. (2004). A lifeline for new teachers. *Educational Leadership, 61*(8), 58–61.

Celiberti, D. A., Bobo, H. E., Kelly, K. S., Harris, S. L., & Handelman, J. S. (1997). The differential and temporal effects of antecedent exercise on the self-stimulatory behavior of a child with autism. *Research in Developmental Disabilities, 18*, 139–150.

Collins, J. (2001). *Good to great.* New York: HarperCollins Publishers Inc.

Conference Board, the Partnership for 21st Century Skills, Corporate Voices for Working Families, & the Society for Human Resource Management. (2006). *Are they really ready to work? Employers' perspectives on the basic knowledge and applied skills of new entrants to the 21st century U.S. workforce.*

Covey, S. (1989). *The seven habits of highly effective people.* New York: Simon & Schuster.

Craft, L. L. & Perna, F. A. (2004). The benefits of exercise for the clinically depressed. *Primary Care Companion of Clinical Psychiatry, 6,* 104–111.

Curwin, R., Mendler, A., & Mendler, B. (2009). *Discipline with dignity (3rd ed.).* Alexandria, VA: ASCD.

Diaz, A. B., & Motta, R. W. (2008). The effects of an aerobic exercise program on post-traumatic stress disorder symptom severity in adolescents. *International Journal of Emergency Mental Health, 10*(1), 49–59.

Duckworth, A., Quinn, P., & Seligman, M. (2009). Positive predictors of teacher effectiveness. *The Journal of Positive Psychology, 4*(6), 540–547.

DuFour, R., DuFour, R., Eaker, R., & Many, T. (2006). *Learning by doing: A handbook for professional learning communities at work.* Bloomington, IN: Solution Tree Press.

Elliott, R. O., Dobbin, A. R., Rose, G. D., & Soper, H. V. (1994). Vigorous aerobic exercise versus general motor activities: Effects on maladaptive and stereotypic behaviors of adults with both autism and mental retardation. *Journal of Autism and Developmental Disorders, 24,* 565–576.

Evanski, G. (2004). *Classroom activators: 64 ways to energize learners.* Thousand Oaks, CA: Corwin.

Feiler, B. (2010). *The council of dads: My daughters, my illness and the men who could be me.* New York: William Morrow, a division of HarperCollins Publishers.

Ferriter, W. M. (2010). Cell phones as teaching tools. *Educational Leadership, 68*(2), 85–86.

Flohr, J. A., Saunders, M. J., Evans, S. W., & Raggi, V. (2004). Effects of physical activity on academic performance and behavior in children with ADHD. *Medicine and Science in Sports and Exercise, 36*(5), S145–S146.

Floriani, V., & Kennedy, C. (2008). Promotion of physical activity in children. *Current Opinion in Pediatrics, 20*(1), 90–95.

Freedman, J. L., & Fraser, S. C. (1966). Compliance without pressure: The foot-in-the-door technique. *Journal of Personality and Social Psychology, 4,* 195–202.

Fullan, M. (2007). *The new meaning of educational change* (4th ed.). New York: Teachers College Press.

Gapin, J., & Etnier, J. (2009). Physical activity and cognitive performance in children with attention deficit hyperactivity disorder (ADHD): Does physical activity participation predict executive function? *Journal of Sport and Exercise Psychology, 31,* 511–512.

Garton, C.. (2010). Companies give in kind, if not in cash. *USA Today,* Monday, August 9, 2010 (Section B), 1–2.

Gladwell, M. (2005). *BLINK: The power of thinking without thinking.* New York: Little, Brown & Company.

Goodlad, J. I. (1994). *Better teachers, better schools.* San Francisco: Jossey-Bass.

Green, C. S., Pouget, A., & Bavelier, D. (2010). Improved probabilistic inference as a general learning mechanism with action video games. *Current Biology, 20*(17), 1573–1579.

Green, E. (2010). Building a better teacher. *New York Times reprints.* www.nytimes.com/2010/03/07/magazine.

Janov, J. (2005). *Managing to stay out of court: How to avoid the 8 deadly sins of mismanagement.* Alexandria, VA & San Francisco, CA: Society for Human Resource Management & Berrett-Koehler Publishers.

Klusmann, U., Kunter, M., Trautwein, U., Ludtke, O., & Baumert, J. (2008). Teachers' occupational well-being and quality of instruction: The important role of self-regulatory patterns. *Journal of Educational Psychology, 100*(3), 702–715.

Kotter, J. P., & Cohen, D. S. (2002). *The heart of change. Real-life stories of how people change their organizations.* Boston: Harvard Business School Press.

Lambert, L. (2003). *Leadership capacity for lasting school improvement.* Alexandria, VA: ASCD.

Lambert, L. (2005). Leadership for lasting reform. *Educational Leadership, 62*(5), 62–65.

Langer, E. J. (1989). Minding matters. In L. Berkowitz (Ed.), *Advances in experimental social psychology, 22.* New York: Academic Press.

Lawlor, D. A., & Hopkins, S. W. (2001). The effectiveness of exercise as an intervention in the management of depression. *British Medical Journal, 322,* 1–8.

Lundin, S. C., Christensen, J., Paul, H., & with Strand, P. (2002). *Fish! Tales.* New York: Hyperion.

Marzano, R. J., Waters, T., & McNulty, B. A. (2005). *School leadership that works.* Alexandria, VA: ASCD.

McKay, M., Davis, M., & Fanning, P. (2007). *Thoughts and feelings: Taking control of your mood and your life.* Oakland, CA: New Harbinger Publications Inc.

Mendler, A. (2006). *Handling difficult parents.* Rochester, NY: Discipline Associates.

Mendler, B. (2009). *The taming of the crew.* Rochester, NY: Discipline Associates.

MetLife survey of the American teacher: Transitions and the role of supportive relationships. (2004–2005). New York: Metropolitan Life Insurance Company.

MetLife survey of the American teacher: Collaborating for student success. (2009). New York: Metropolitan Life Insurance Company.

Miner, A. G., Glomb, T. M., & Hulin, C. (2005). Experience sampling mood and its correlates at work: Diary studies in workplace psychology. *Journal of Occupational and Organizational Psychology, 78*(2), 171–193.

Otake, K., Shimai, S., & Fredrickson, B. L. (2006). Happy people become happier through kindness: A counting kindness intervention. *Journal of Happiness Studies, 7*(3), 361–375.

Patterson, K., Grenny, J., Maxfield, D., McMillan, R., & Switzler, A. (2008). *Influencer: The power to change anything.* New York McGraw-Hill.

Pink, D. (2009). *Drive: The surprising truth about what motivates us.* New York: Riverhead Books.

Pitts, L. (2011, June 5). Live for the end. *The Plain Dealer.*

Reeves, D. B. *Transforming professional development into student results.* (2010). Alexandria, VA: ASCD.

Rosenthal-Malek, A., & Mitchell, S. (1997). The effects of exercise on the self-stimulatory behaviors and positive responding of adolescents with autism. *Journal of Autism and Developmental Disabilities, 27,* 193–202.

Saphier, J. (2005). *John Adams' promise: How to have good schools for all our children, not just for some.* Acton, MA: Research for Better Teaching.

Scott, E. (2011). Health benefits of laughter: Stress relief, immunity and more. www.about.com (updated January 10, 2011).

Seligman, M., Steen, T. A., Park, N., & Peterson, C. (2005). Positive psychology progress: Empirical validation of interventions. *American Psychologist, 60*(5), 410–421.

Shepard, R. J. (1997). Curricular physical activity and academic performance. *Pediatric Exercise Science, 9,* 113–126.

Smith, A. (2010). Technology trends among people of color. *Pew Internet & American Life Project.* www.pewinternet.org. Sept. 17, 2010.

Stahl, S. M. (2008). *Essential psychopharmacology, 3rd ed.: Neuroscientific basis and practical application.* New York: Cambridge University Press.

Stock, G. (2004). *The kids' book of questions.* New York: Workman Publishing.

Swingle, C. (2011, February 25). *Trip of best days.* Rochester Democrat & Chronicle, p. A1.

Tomporowski, P. D., Davis, C. L., Miller, P. H., & Naglieri, J. A. (2008). Exercise and children's intelligence, cognition, and academic achievement. *Educational Psychology Review, 20,* 111–131.

Trim, D. (2010). *I am thankful for my challenging students.* www.inside the school.com/articles i-am-thankful-for-my-challenging-students.

U.S. Census Bureau (2009). *Educational attainment in the United States: 2007.* Retrieved from www.census.gov/prod/2009pubs/p20-560.pdf.

Wells, M. M. (2000). Office clutter or meaningful personal displays: The role of office personalization in employee and organizational well-being. *Journal of Environmental Psychology, 20,* 239–255.

Whitaker, T., & Fiore D. J. (2001). *Dealing with difficult parents.* Larchmont, NY: Eye on Education.

Wolk, S. (2001). The benefits of exploratory time. *Educational Leadership, 59*(2), 56–59.

Yuen, S. (2005). *The three virtues of effective parenting.* Rutland, VT: Tuttle Publishing.

Zavadsky, H. (2010). *Bringing school reform to scale.* Boston: Harvard Education Press.

Index

The letter *f* following a page number denotes a figure.

About the Author

Allen Mendler, Ph.D., is an educator and school psychologist who resides in Rochester, New York. He has worked extensively with children of all ages in regular and special education settings. Dr. Mendler has consulted with many schools and day and residential centers, including extensive work with youth in juvenile detention. Dr. Mendler's emphasis is on developing effective frameworks and strategies for educators, youth professionals, and parents to help difficult youth succeed. As one of the internationally acclaimed authors of the original and newly revised *Discipline with Dignity*, Dr. Mendler has given many workshops and seminars to professionals and parents. He is highly acclaimed as a motivational speaker and trainer for numerous educational organizations. Dr. Mendler is the author or co-author of 15 books, including *Power Struggles 2nd Edition: Successful Techniques for Educators, Motivating Students Who Don't Care, Connecting with Students, Handling Difficult Parents, Strategies for Successful Classroom Management* and the *What Do I Do When?* series. His articles have appeared in many journals, including *Educational Leadership, Kappan,* and *Reclaiming Children and Youth.* Dr. Mendler has been recognized for his distinguished teaching by the Bureau of Education and

Research and was a recipient of the coveted Crazy Horse Award for making outstanding contributions to discouraged youth. For speaking and seminar engagements, Dr. Mendler can be reached at 800-772-5227 or tlc-sems.com.

Related ASCD Resources: Effective Teachers

At the time of publication, the following ASCD resources were available (ASCD stock numbers appear in parentheses). For up-to-date information about ASCD resources, go to www.ascd.org.

Print Products

The Art and Science of Teaching: A Comprehensive Framework for Effective Instruction by Robert J. Marzano (#107001)

Connecting with Students by Allen N. Mendler (#101236)

Discipline with Dignity by Richard L. Curwin, Allen N. Mendler, and Brian D. Mendler (#108036)

Educational Leadership, March 2006: Improving Professional Practice (Entire Issue #106041)

Everyday Engagement: Making Students and Parents Your Partners in Learning by Katy Ridnouer (#109009)

Handbook for Enhancing Professional Practice: Using the Framework for Teaching in Your School by Charlotte Danielson (#106035)

Handbook for Qualities of Effective Teachers by James H. Stronge, Pamela D. Tucker, and Jennifer L. Hindman (#104135)

How to Give Effective Feedback to Your Students by Susan M. Brookhart (#108019)

Improving Student Learning One Teacher at a Time by Jane E. Pollock (#107005)

Qualities of Effective Teachers, 2nd Edition by James H. Stronge (#105156)

Online Courses

Classroom Management: Building Effective Relationships: An ASCD PD Online Course (#PD11OC104)

Videos and DVDs

Qualities of Effective Teachers (three video programs on one DVD, plus a facilitator's guide) (#604423)

A Visit to Classrooms of Effective Teachers (one 45-minute DVD with a comprehensive viewer's guide) (DVD #605026; Video #405026)

THE WHOLE CHILD The Whole Child Initiative helps schools and communities create learning environments that allow students to be healthy, safe, engaged, supported, and challenged. To learn more about other books and resources that relate to the whole child, visit www.wholechildeducation.org.

For more information: send e-mail to member@ascd.org; call 1-800-933-2723 or 703-578-9600, press 1; send a fax to 703-575-5400; or write to Information Services, ASCD, 1703 N. Beauregard St., Alexandria, VA 22311-1714 USA.